ABOUT THE AUTHOR

Declan Dunne is a journalist who works at RTÉ. His previous book, *Peter's Key: Peter DeLoughry and the Fight for Irish Independence*, was also published by Mercier Press.

MULLIGAN'S

Grand Old Pub of Poolbeg Street

Declan Dunne

MERCIER PRESS

IRISH PUBLISHER – IRISH STORY

MERCIER PRESS

Cork

www.mercierpress.ie

ISBN: 978 1 78117 348 0

10 9 8 7 6 5 4 3 2 1

A CIP record for this title is available from the British Library

Printed and bound in the EU.

CONTENTS

To

Joan, Joseph, Sarah and Shane Grogan
and their extended family

www.facebook.com/careforshane

Acknowledgements

I owe particular thanks to Peter Roche, who supplied many documents and nuggets of information concerning Mulligan's. The Cusack families were unflaggingly supportive of the project throughout.

Many individuals offered their knowledge of Mulligan's in varying measure, all of whom deserve my gratitude: Denis Bannister, Matt and Tina Bannon, Ronnie Bellew, John Boland, Tony Byrne, David Carr, Mike Carr, Declan Cassidy, James Cassidy, Moira Cassidy, John Channing, Jim and Lisa Culligan, Peter Donovan, Charles 'Doc' Dougherty, Colman Doyle, Ian Doyle, Wynn Dunne, Julian P. Foynes, Natalie Gardner, Evelyn and Paul Gethings, Anthony Grealish, Oliver Grealish, Liz Heffernan, Brian Igoe, Fergal Kearns, John Kelly, Joe Kennedy, Peter Kilbride, Margaret Kinsella, Chuck Kinslow, Jack Law, Ciarán Lenoach, Richard Levins, Tom McCaughren, Eileen McDonald, Bob McGuirk, Eoin McKevitt, Martin Mannion, John Menaghan, Jon Monroe, Martine Murphy, Michael Murphy, Dermot Nolan of Dixon McGaver Nolan Architects, Jack O'Donohoe, Maureen O'Flaherty, Jer O'Leary, Mary O'Neill, Ed O'Neill, Terry O'Sullivan, John Quirke of John Quirke Photography, Vincent Reddin, Desiree Short, Micheál Smyth, Robert Sweeney, Imelda and Paul Swords, Joseph F. Wakelee-Lynch, Tom Wall, Jimmy Walsh, Ken Whelan and Darragh Wilson.

Historians and archivists who gave their time and expertise greatly enhanced the history and understanding of Mulligan's: Turtle Bunbury; Raelene Casey, Moving Image Access Officer, Irish Film Institute; Dr Mary Clarke, City Archivist, Dublin City Archive; Joy Conley, Media Research Associates, Inc., Noyes Drive, Silver Spring, Maryland, USA; Tim Pat Coogan; Derek Cullen, Fáilte Ireland; Niall Dardis, Archivist, Dublin Port & Docks; Pastor Corinna Diestelkamp, Lutheran Church of Ireland; Noelle Dowling, Dublin Diocesan Archives; Conor Doyle, theatre historian; Paul Ferguson, Map Librarian, Trinity College Library, Dublin; Professor R. F. Foster, Carroll Professor of Irish History at Hertford College, Oxford; the Glasnevin Trust; Máire Harris, Irish Film Archive; Sara Hawran, Research Room, John F. Kennedy Library, Columbia Point, Boston, Massachusetts, USA; Bernie Kane, Licensed Vintners Association, Dublin; A. P. Kearns; Colm Lennon; Elizabeth McEvoy, National Archives of Ireland; Elaine McManus, The Sick and Indigent Room-keepers' Society, Dublin; Jennifer Moore, Royal Irish Academy; Brian Murphy, photographic archivist; Robert Nicholson, Secretary, James Joyce Centre, Dublin; Senator David Norris; Gregory O'Connor, National Archives of Ireland; Dr Riana O'Dwyer; Kieran O'Leary, Irish Film Archive; Colum O'Riordan, Archive Administrator, Irish Architectural Archive; Carmel Rice, Meath Heritage Centre; Registry of Deeds, Henrietta Street, Dublin; Irene Stevenson, Librarian, Digital Archive, *The Irish Times*; Whyte's Auctioneers, Dublin.

I owe special thanks to the photographer, Cyril Byrne; to the Board of Trinity College for allowing reproduction of a section of Rocque's map in Trinity College Library, Dublin; and to the journalist and author Paul Williams.

The staff of Mulligan's, past and present, were all extremely helpful to the research that formed the basis for this book: Luke China, Dave Cregan, Lorraine Doyle, Jeff Harris, Noel Hawkins, Christy Hynes, Mick Murray, Billy Phelan, Danny Tracey, Con and Brigid Cusack, Gary Cusack, his wife, Cari Mooney, Carmel and Ger Cusack, their son, Darran, and daughter, Shauna, Evelyn Cusack, P. J. (Paddy) Kelly and Seán O'Donohoe.

Ray Burke, senior news editor, RTÉ, John S. Doyle, Dr Martin Holland and David McCullagh, the historian and RTÉ *Prime Time* presenter, went to great lengths to help me refine and improve early drafts of the manuscript. Their advice and knowledge left me enthralled and humbled.

Any errors or omissions in the text are mine alone.

Finally, no work of this magnitude can be concluded without the encouragement given to me by many of those mentioned above. I also owe a great deal to the knowledge and friendship of Nan Budinger, Charlie Collins and Mary Dunne of Collins Photo Agency, Matt Leech, John Levins, Mary Long, William 'Spud' Murphy and Richard Whyte.

Declan Dunne
Dublin, 2015

A Note on the Text

The nature of the business carried on in previous times on the premises that Mulligan's occupies is difficult to establish. It is described as a spirit grocer from its establishment in 1782 right up to the 1960s. These traders were forbidden to allow alcohol to be consumed on the premises but were allowed to sell it. Throughout the 1800s temperance campaigners, politicians and owners of other forms of licensed premises complained about spirit grocers violating the law. It is likely that one of the first owners of the premises, Talbot Fyan, was one of the many spirit grocers who ran what we know today as a pub, even though this was against the law.

The evidence for this is more tantalising than telling. A legal document from the 1850s describes Fyan's establishment as 'a well-known and long established grocery and vintner's establishment'. A court report in the 1860s, when John Mulligan ran the business, includes reference to a man drinking on the premises. It is more likely that both Fyan and Mulligan, under their separate ownerships, operated the outlet as a pub similar to other spirit grocers. The term spirit grocer, then, has to be treated carefully. It is used in the text but it is important to bear in mind that while Mulligan's was a spirit grocer by name, it was, at least from the 1860s onwards, a pub by nature.

There is also the question of when the business ceased to

be a grocery. Remnants of the business can be seen in Mulligan's today. In the front bar there are hooks embedded in the ceiling which may have been used to hold scales or baskets of fruit and vegetables. Working backwards, no one who frequented Mulligan's and who was interviewed for this book can remember fruit or vegetables being sold on the premises in the 1950s. However, in the 1960s headed notepaper was used by one of the owners on which was printed, 'John Mulligan & Son, Grocers, Tea, Wine & Spirit Merchants'. Again, this is scant evidence, as the date this headed notepaper was originally printed is not known.

The schedules of assets from the wills of two previous owners, Michael Smith, who died in 1962, and James Mulligan, son of John Mulligan, who died in 1931, list many items on the premises but none bearing any relation to the grocery trade. A newspaper report of a bird flying into Mulligan's in 1934 tells of it being given some seed, an indication that goods other than alcohol were then sold on the premises. When Talbot Fyan sold the premises in 1844, a list of items to be auctioned including furniture and fittings was published in *The Freeman's Journal*, but again there is nothing there to suggest that a grocery was part of the business.

INTRODUCTION

In 2012 a man went into Mulligan's and asked the barman, Gary Cusack, if he could see Billy. Thinking that the customer was referring to another barman, Billy 'Swiss' Phelan, Gary said that he was on holiday. 'No, not that Billy,' the man replied, 'I mean Billy in the clock.'

Billy Brooks Carr from Houston, Texas, who died in 2011, regarded the pint of Guinness in Mulligan's so highly that his brothers had some of his ashes flown 4,500 miles to Ireland where they were deposited in the base of the grandfather clock in Mulligan's bar. His family and friends continue to make pilgrimages to Mulligan's to drink a toast to his life and memory.

This is just one of the fascinating connections that Mulligan's has with the extraordinary, where distance and death are no obstacles. There are also links between the pub and Judy Garland, James Joyce, John F. Kennedy, British monarchs, Napoleon Bonaparte, the Oscar-winning film *My Left Foot*, Flann O'Brien, Peter O'Toole, Eusebio, the birth of rock and roll and a raid by the Black and Tans. These names and events might have been plucked out of an encyclopaedia, but all have found themselves in the index of this book.

No other building on earth has had within it the star of the *Wizard of Oz*, the 'Camelot' president and the author of *Ulysses*. It has also been the unlikely scene of extraordinary events over its more than 230-year history: unlikely, because it is off the beaten path; unlikely, because its owners and staff down the years have not sought to attract attention; and unlikely because it has been, generally, impervious to change.

The pub also remains beneath the radar of encyclopaedias and is not given prominence in official lists of tourist sites. Despite all this, Mulligan's is known and loved by hundreds of thousands of people around the world.

Quirkiness may be the key to the extent of Mulligan's renown and notoriety. It is an unscientific matter, quirkiness, but Mulligan's has managed to bottle it and uncork it in large measure. The quirkiness is built into the bricks and mortar, pervades its atmosphere and rises from its cellars.

Mulligan's does not have universal appeal. While it might provide the connoisseur's pint of Guinness, it is not everyone's cup of tea. Indeed, some former regulars speak of only the negative aspects of the pub. The reasons for this have more than one root. In the past, the great trade that the pub enjoyed meant that barmen, on occasion, did not have time to engage in over-the-counter conversations; this annoyed some customers who liked to chat. The rules in Mulligan's, such as the ban on singing and its strict abhorrence of unsavoury or over-excited conversations, do not suit all the customers. Some staff, in the past, who did not always obey the normal rules of courtesy, enjoyed exceptional loyalty from the owners. While this aspect of the pub annoyed some customers, who wanted errant barmen to be reprimanded by their bosses, others thought it intriguing and even found humour in the outbursts of brusqueness. While its bartenders today are regarded as exponents of courtesy, in years gone by some were devoid of this quality, or appeared to be devoid of it until customers got to know and appreciate their ways. They were what might be called 'characters', a description that, in Ireland at least, kindly absolves such people of all blame for breaches of convention.

The relationship in Mulligan's between bartenders and customers rests on at least two levels, based on how well they know each other. First-time visitors might find the dynamics whirling about the premises fascinating or off-putting, depending on what moves them. Then there are the regulars. Familiarity, in the case of Mulligan's, breeds contest: who can outdo the other in mischief?

An example of this involved Mick Murray from Finglas in Dublin, who began working in the pub in 2001. One of the regulars, nicknamed 'The Minister', whose job it was to open and shut the doors of a nearby office, used to slip in and out of the pub during his shift. Before returning to work, he used to place a beer mat on top of his unfinished pint of Guinness as a sign that he would be returning to it, a practice akin to territorial swimmers stabbing the stem of their large beach umbrella into the sand. One day he returned from the lavatory to take a sup from his pint at the bar and found it would not lift off the counter. He was unaware that Mick Murray had glued the bottom of the glass to a beer mat and glued the beer mat to the counter. 'The Minister' tried a couple of times to release the pint, looking around before each attempt, afraid that he might call attention to himself. No one appeared to be taking any notice of him. Time was getting on. He had to return to work and so he put a beer mat on top of his pint, indicating he would be back. While he was gone, Mick used a scraper to release the pint from the stuck-down beer mat, and the beer mat from the counter. Less than five minutes later, 'The Minister' returned and found his pint still in place. A little nervously, he removed the beer mat he had placed on top of the pint and looked around. Other customers were chatting, minding their own business. He relaxed. He put his two hands around the bottom of the glass and checked that he was not being watched. Then he applied himself to his predicament, taking a moment before he wrenched the pint off the counter, only to find that it came away easily and at a ferocious speed. The contents shot out of the glass, over his shoulder, splashing and thus 'baptising' two tourists on their first visit to Mulligan's.

The following day 'The Minister' returned to find that someone had turned his pint upside down on the bar, with the Guinness vacuum-locked inside. Having taken advice from other customers, he tried to retrieve his Guinness by slowly sliding the pint off the bar onto a beer mat to stop the stout escaping but, again, it splashed onto the floor. 'The Minister' threatened to report the interference with his pints to the co-owner, Tommie Cusack, but never did.

It is interesting that 'The Minister' did not complain. He stayed quiet because he knew he was in a world where jousting in mischief was to be expected, to be challenged and, if possible, to be defeated. The mark of the glued beer mat remains on the counter in the bar, a testament to one of the more unusual phenomena found in the pub – 'Mulliganarchy'. Within this small universe, however, there also exists professionalism and efficiency, as exemplified by the owners and staff, including the redoubtable Mick Murray.

Among the barmen, Noel Hawkins manages to convey irrepressible good form and serve as much wit as he does drink, even on the most trying of nights in Mulligan's. His reservoir of jokes consistently drowns customers in tears of laughter. He can hold his own with any off-the-cuff stand-up comedian. Noel became well known for calling time by reminding the many customers from Trinity College: 'Now, come on students, mind your grants.' This was generally uttered as he waged war on the carpet armed with a vacuum cleaner. Tourists in particular enjoy his constant repartee. On one occasion in the 1990s, a group of visitors from the United States ordered several Irish coffees. As the high maintenance beverages were being prepared, one of the group, in an attempt to make conversation, said: 'We came in here in 1980', to which Noel replied: 'I'm serving as fast as I can.'

Christy Hynes is also known for his high level of wit. He commands the respect and admiration of colleague and customer alike for his bar skills, and his deep interest in people and the world about him. However, there is one aspect of him that is rarely commented upon – his mastery of discharging a long, rambling request for drinks. This is generally submitted by an indecisive customer, continuing consultations with his entourage while placing his order. Christy deals with such challenges unflappably by sweeping his hands into action, selecting glasses, pouring drinks, uncapping tonic bottles, re-affirming the order, unloading ice and placing beer mats. At the appropriate time, he might ask the customer whether he has a twenty or fifty cent coin to avoid delay in foraging for change. Notes are handed over as the coin is passed, Guinness taps are lifted and the transaction is concluded with the crisp command – 'Next.'

The task involves highly tuned motor skills, split-second decision-making on the sequence of drinks to be dispensed and a mathematical turn. Sometimes all this has to be carried out at the same time as the barmen hear a knock from the cellar hatch cut into the floor area, warning them that it is about to be opened. Christy overcomes this extra obstacle by deftly stepping around the plunge-threatening drop, not allowing it to interfere with the fluidity of the operation. The entire manoeuvre is executed with precision and versatility, proving that these qualities are not unique to a Bernstein, a Nureyev or an Einstein.

Billy 'Swiss' Phelan is wont to bless himself on seeing certain customers or utter phrases of foreboding such as 'most merciful' and 'here's trouble'. Customers at the upper end of Mulligan's warning scale might hear him use the code phrase 'Lán gealach' (Irish for full moon) to another barman, alerting him that a touch of madness might ensue. Other customers, who have consumed more than their usual quota of drink, may hear him say 'full of rubber' as he passes by, or, if they have been deserted by their drinking partners, 'Two down, one to go.'

Mulligan's, for stalwart GAA (Gaelic Athletic Association) fans, becomes the centre of the universe after All-Irelands, a favourite day for Danny Tracey. The pub is a good twenty-minute walk from Croke Park, where finals are held. On All-Ireland days, the pub becomes the neutral corner for rival supporters. Poolbeg Street turns into a mosaic of team colours as the spillover from Mulligan's engulfs the area. Inside, supporters of one team discuss the minutiae of the game with supporters from opposing teams. Similarities to previous games are plucked from memories and put forward. Teenage sons and daughters look on and listen to the conversations. Younger children with soft drinks and crisps make their way through the throng of adults.

Danny Tracey describes such days as mayhem, but looks upon them fondly, particularly the Dublin All-Ireland football victories over Kerry in 2011 and Mayo in 2013: 'They were extraordinary. I don't think there was a tap vertical for eight hours. In 2011 the system crashed in the place, the cooler couldn't cope.'

Darran Cusack has inherited the cheeky and, at times, scathing wit of his father, Ger, and his grandfather, Tommie. His interest in golf and Manchester United draws him, at times, into conflict or camaraderie with customers, depending on their own sporting loyalties. One of the tasks he relishes is the weekly winding of the grandfather clock, which is done with reverence and a quiet word to Billy Brooks Carr, whose ashes lie within its frame.

Mulligan's is known for serving the best pint of Guinness in the world. Darran Cusack explained why the pub continues to enjoy this reputation:

Some of the reasons I've heard over the years have been the short draw on the line from the keg to the tap. There is less than two pints in our lines. Glass management is a big factor because we don't wash our glasses in dish washers. They are rinsed with fresh water all the time. It's not recycled water. We don't do food so we don't have greasy glasses and we deep-clean them every six or seven weeks so that's a huge factor. We store the Guinness in batches of thirty kegs. In the cold room at any time there could be ninety. We use one batch at a time.

He cites one last factor, delivered with a twinkle in his eye: 'Of course, you need a good barman as well.'

Mulligan's latest recruit at the time of writing, lounge attendant Luke China, has adapted well to the daily life of the pub, despite coming from a very different culture. He returns to his native Dalian in north-east China for a month every two years, but has found in Mulligan's 'a home away from home'. He has earned the respect of the staff and customers for his work ethic. He regularly posts cartoons of customers on his Facebook page and endures with good grace the onslaught of teasing from them about his beloved team, Manchester United. Humour and sport have become a special hybrid language of communication between him and the locals. In the world of Mulligan's, what is foreign or different does not become a stumbling block to human interaction, but is embraced.

The Mulligan's enterprise is overseen by the Cusack brothers, Gary and Ger (Darran's father), who are much amused by the daily fascinations the pub offers. 'Only in Mulligan's' is a phrase much used by them. Aside from the rich mix of people drawn to the pub, there always appears to be something going on. Both Gary and Ger enjoy relating, or learning about, wacky episodes in the long-running Mulligan's drama. Neither is generally capable of keeping a straight face when talking about the many capers generated on the premises. Aside from appreciating and encouraging this colourful aspect of the business, Gary and Ger also apply, to a great degree, the skills of the licensed trade taught to them by their father, Tommie, their uncle, Con, and several bartenders who have worked for them. All this has made them effective curators of the grand old pub of Poolbeg Street.

While Mulligan's enjoys a greater mixture of custom than its suburban counterparts, some of its barmen used to find the repetitive questioning about the pub's reputation and history exasperating. Paddy Kelly, who started working in the pub in the mid-1980s and was there for twelve years, recalled a conversation during which one of his colleagues was asked a succession of such questions, which were met by the curt response: 'Oh, yeah.' The questioner was not sure if this should be interpreted as a 'Yes' or whether it was suggesting some doubt about their own assumptions. However, even this most world-weary of exchanges in Mulligan's managed to throw up an unexpected ending:

> *Tourist:* We've heard Mulligan's is the oldest pub in Ireland. Is that right?
>
> *Barman:* Oh, yeah.
>
> *Tourist:* We've heard James Joyce used to drink here? Is that right?
>
> *Barman:* Oh, yeah.
>
> *Tourist:* Does Mulligan's have the best pint of Guinness in Ireland?
>
> *Barman:* I wouldn't know about that. I only drink brandy myself.

Mulligan's was, and is, an imperfect institution. Nowadays, it is quite normal for people to smile when the name Mulligan's is mentioned. It conjures up a mixture of mischief, the frailty of human nature and the richness of humour all wrapped up in an Irishness beloved by native and foreigner alike. The goings-on between opening and closing times have inspired great writers and have attracted some of the most famous people over the past two centuries or so. Its doors remain open despite all that life and myopic Dublin city planners have thrown at it.

This book opens a centuries-old drawer to reveal the sparkling history of a globally-known business. The lives, tragedies and ways of its owners and staff are portrayed, and the capers, stories and history of its customers, famous, infamous and ordinary, are told on the pages that follow. We shall also see the parts played by the pub in historic events. The narrative focuses on the world through the Mulligan's lens. Certainly, this is an unusual way to view the past, but one that, I hope, will add an extra layer of truth. Through this Mulligan's microscope, the reader will see previously hidden aspects of Dublin, of Ireland, of the world, of famous people, of ordinary people and, indeed, of life itself.

The institution has earned its place in the world; while China boasts of its Great Wall, New York the Statue of Liberty and Paris the Eiffel Tower, Dublin is bejewelled by Mulligan's on Poolbeg Street.

Further information about Mulligan's can be found on the website accompanying this book: www.mulligansbook. com.

1

Counter Hatched

Before Mulligan's existed, before alcohol could be stocked, served or sipped on the premises, another liquid had to be drained and barred from the neighbourhood. The River Liffey regularly overflowed onto the north and south banks of Dublin city in the late seventeenth and early eighteenth centuries, wetting the spirit for trade and whetting the appetite for complaints to the municipal authorities. The ground from which Mulligan's would rise was boggy and pool-ridden, attracting fishermen who profited from the worms they chivvied out of the mudflats.

In the early 1700s William Mercer, a merchant, began to fill in and stabilise the land from Lazar's Hill (also known as Lazy Hill and Lazer's Hill, now called Townsend Street) to George's Quay. Poolbeg Street – lying parallel to the river and one block south of it – was to become one of the gridded thoroughfares laid out on this virgin parcel of land in the early years of the eighteenth century.[1] Mercer's work, along with separate projects undertaken by Dublin Corporation and another developer, Sir John Rogerson, reclaimed large areas of estuary land and 'quayed in' the area, corralling the river to halt the watery incursions.[2]

Families, builders and other tradespeople drifted onto the newly formed patch of ground, among them a block-maker, Nicholas Schults, who wasted no time in making his mark on the landscape.[3] He embarked on a flurry of construction, engaging in several property transactions in the vicinity over three decades.[4] One of these occurred on 20 March 1750, when he took possession of a house from a shipwright, William Murphy.[5] It shared a cellar with another building. They would, in time, become Nos 8 and 9: Mulligan's of Poolbeg Street. These premises were among dozens that sprang up on the street in the 1700s. Both buildings have stood for well over two centuries, defying time, tide and tirade.

The year 1782 is emblazoned on a beam in Mulligan's bar, denoting when the original grocery business began on the premises.[6] Moses Walsh was listed as a grocer there in 1784, but not before that. However, the local directory listings were not always up to date and there is strong evidence to suggest he was the first owner-occupier of the business premises known today as Mulligan's. The year 1782 was also an eventful one for Talbot and Mary Fyan, who were relatives of Moses Walsh and his wife, Catherine. The Fyans had a son, also called Moses.[7] The boy, like his biblical namesake, benefited, as did everyone else in Poolbeg Street, from the river being kept in check. The Fyans took over the business from the Walshes in 1787.[8] However, the Walshes left one more record that year before disappearing from the pages of history. They, too, had a son who was called after his father.[9]

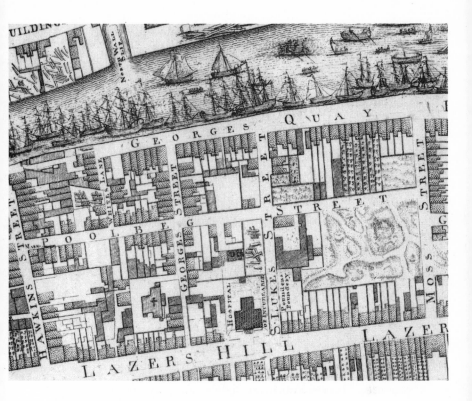

While the Red Sea had only one Moses to contend with, the penned-in Liffey faced three. It kept its distance and Poolbeg Street thrived. Through hard work, the families tried to ensure that their children would live to see and enjoy the benefits their promised land might bring.

By 1787, when the Fyans began selling fruit, vegetables and spirits, Poolbeg Street had been in existence for well over half a century and had developed a distinct, if quirky, personality.[10] Part of this was formed by the street's proximity to the Liffey, seen crowded with sailing ships, rowing boats, schooners and other craft in John Rocque's map of Dublin (1756) above. This traffic led to a plethora of warehouses, coal merchants and corn dealers operating in Poolbeg Street and its vicinity. One writer noted that 'the reclaimed ground became peopled by sailors and the hardy classes'.[11]

As a street of unremarkable dimensions (more comfortable with single-lane modern traffic and about the length of three soccer pitches), Poolbeg Street still managed to provide the setting for remarkable displays of pantomime, farce, comedy and tragedy.[12] It was eccentric, exotic and even mystical. It exuded an air of earthiness and theatricality, brimming with oddballs, inventors, biscuit makers, villains, corn dealers and a well-known porcelain seller known as the 'Emperor of China'.[13]

Despite stiff competition, Talbot Fyan emerged as one of the more prominent curiosities of Poolbeg Street. To begin to understand him, it is necessary to explore his surroundings, and what better way to do this than to stand beside him outside his shop in the first years of his stewardship to see who and what we might find.

Dozens of Dutch Lutherans are walking by. They, like the French Huguenot community, are in Ireland because of persecution for their faith in their homeland. The presence of the Dutch Lutherans in the vicinity explains the reason for a strong continental influence. Fyan, a Roman Catholic, nods at them as they pass. He respects other faiths.

Poolbeg Street had the appearance of a little Amsterdam, lined with buildings whose frontages mimicked a characteristic of that city where the roofs are masked by quadrants sweeping up to pediments. The feature gives the impression of a series of waves travelling horizontally across the building-tops with semi-circular troughs punctuated by triangular, flat or curved peaks. This architectural serenity – known as a Dutch Billy – was prevalent in other areas of Dublin, but particularly so in Poolbeg Street; the building occupied by Fyan, No. 8, was one of several Dutch Billys gracing the street.[14]

The guttural burr of Dutch diminishes. The Lutherans have passed by and we can make out their destination at the eastern end of Poolbeg Street. They are heading towards the Dutch church, a brick box of a building, which seats 400 worshippers and eschews decoration.[15] The church attracted Dutch immigrants, including builders, merchants and sailors, to the area.[16]

Despite the size of the building, the community was small and their church had little money. Their minister, John George Frederick Schulze, compensated for his lack of income by conducting irregular marriages where no banns were called and no licence obtained. His registers show that he conducted up to 6,000 such marriages in Poolbeg Street between 1806 and 1837.[17]

Another institution stands at the western end of the street, at the junction with Hawkins Street. This is the repository of the Dublin Society, which includes a library occupying three rooms. Its exhibition room is 'lofty and spacious, the light being so disposed from the roof as to display the paintings to the best effect, and, next to the Louvre, it was considered the finest of its kind in Europe'.[18]

The presence of the Dublin Society's holdings gave Poolbeg Street a scientific edge. Its model-maker, Robert Hall, and a mathematical instrument-maker, Thomas Hicks, lived on the street.[19] So too did a timber merchant, Philip Levi Hodgson, whose textbook on measuring became a standard work running into several editions.[20] Other Poolbeg Street residents were the society's husbandry artist, John Fyans, and an engraver, John Mannin, described as 'a valuable artist who does honour to his country'.[21] However, the most celebrated practitioner of the fine arts in the area was James Donovan, who was known as the 'Emperor of China' because of his china and glassware establishment in Poolbeg Street, which extended all the way down to George's Quay.[22]

From his doorway, Talbot Fyan spots one of his neighbours, a house-painter, Thomas Traynor, who has achieved some celebrity.[23] He was the first witness called for the defence in a case taken against Dr William Drennan, a campaigner for Irish independence and a close friend of Theobald Wolfe Tone. Drennan was charged with committing seditious libel. Traynor's evidence was so clear and forceful that the prosecutor felt it best not to cross-examine him and told him to leave the witness box. Drennan was eventually cleared.[24] A more famous campaigner for Irish independence, James Napper Tandy, one of the founders of the Society of United Irishmen, has a house and garden across the street from Fyan's establishment.[25]

Politics in the first two decades of Fyan's business consumed debate in the country. Grattan's parliament was established in 1782, the year in which the business housing Mulligan's today was founded. The Rebellion of 1798, the Act of Union 1801 and the Rebellion of 1803 fed conversations in Fyan's shop and elsewhere. Napper Tandy was sentenced to death in 1801 for treason, but was saved from execution. It is reputed that Napoleon Bonaparte intervened vigorously on his behalf and made Tandy's release a condition of the French signing a peace accord (Treaty of Amiens, 1802) with the British.[26] This provides the first, if tenuous, connection between an owner of Nos 8 and 9 Poolbeg Street and a globally known figure. Talbot Fyan could always say after 1802 that he once had a neighbour who was saved from the gallows by Napoleon.

Sailors, who have just disembarked, are walking down Poolbeg Street singing shanties; some are fighting. There is the smell of fish as another crate of herring is being delivered. Someone screams down the street as a coal delivery claims a finger. Talbot Fyan rubs his chin. He is worried. He does not have enough money and nor does anyone else. He then becomes cheerful: he has figured out a solution devised from the many elements apparent in Poolbeg Street – ingenuity, craftsmanship and a slight touch of rebellion. He is going to mint his own coinage.

Part of the reason for this decision was likely to have been prompted by the size to which his family had grown. He needed every penny. By the mid-1790s Mary Fyan had given birth to eight children. The family had been operating their business from No. 9, but now decided to operate from No. 8.

It is likely that this exchange coincided with the removal of two large fireplaces to make more room for a trading area in the new shop, No. 8, and the marking of one of the beams – which was necessary for the conversion – with the legend 'Est. 1782'.

The shortage of small-denomination coins in the 1790s was the reason why Talbot Fyan decided to issue his own currency in the form of half-penny tokens. These were used in place of official money but were accepted as legal tender by customers and traders, who knew they were always redeemable from the seller. Two of the inscriptions chosen by Fyan for his coins were: 'May Ireland ever flourish' and 'For the honor [sic] and use of trade'. These inscriptions point towards Fyan's patriotism, which became evident in later years. His decision to have the barter coins struck showed that he had an adventurous and entrepreneurial bent. His business acumen, however, was tested by the area in which he lived.

At that time many parts of Dublin were the source of newspaper reports of burglaries, muggings and physical assaults. Poolbeg Street, however, held a particular attraction for criminals. After a young man was robbed of cash at knife-point on Poolbeg Street, *The Freeman's Journal* noted that 'several houses in that street have long been receptacles for the profligates and want much to be visited by the high sheriffs'.[27] Fyan's was one of several premises raided when 'villains ... stole several articles out of his shop'.[28]

Aside from crime, another aspect of the street that

hindered the promotion of business was poverty. A survey at the start of the nineteenth century found that Poolbeg Street had an average of twelve residents in each of its forty-two houses, indicating that it could hold its own with the jungle of tenements elsewhere in the city.[29]

In 1806 Mary Fyan gave birth to her twelfth child, Talbot. Despite the responsibilities linked to supporting such a large family, along with safeguarding his business against crime, Talbot Fyan launched himself into several charitable enterprises. His activities extended to championing political causes and promoting commerce in the city, which linked him with the leading Irish politician of the age, Daniel O'Connell.

Fyan was a member of and fund-raiser for the Charitable Society for the Relief of Sick and Indigent Room-Keepers, which helped 'the most pitiable objects of distress' and was 'unusually for its time, a non-sectarian, non-denominational organisation and it often went to great lengths to emphasise this virtue'.[30] He was president of the society that ran the St Andrew's parish orphanages from 1806 to 1808. The orphans were 'dieted, lodged, clothed, educated and, when qualified, apprenticed to respectable trades'.[31] Fyan's charity work involved raising subscriptions for schools for destitute children, one of which was built in Poolbeg Street.[32] He was mentioned in newspaper reports on two occasions as having worked directly with Daniel O'Connell to collect funds for poverty-stricken children.[33]

Fyan's grocery business received an enormous boost in

1816 when work commenced on construction of the Corn Exchange, an impressive building that stretched from Burgh Quay to Poolbeg Street, following approval of the design by the Wide Streets Commission.[34] The exchange attracted thousands of merchants and traders to deal in cereal grains. It was also used in later times by Daniel O'Connell as a centre for agitation and to hold large meetings as part of his campaign for Catholic emancipation. Nearby businesses (including Fyan's spirit grocery, which was five doors up from the back entrance of the Exchange) benefited greatly from the crowds it attracted. The opening of the Theatre Royal on the corner of Poolbeg Street and Hawkins Street in 1821 also brought significant numbers of both daytime and evening customers to Fyan's shop.[35] King George IV visited the Theatre Royal in August of that year, shortly after ascending the throne.[36]

In spite of the extra demands that the Corn Exchange and charity work placed on Fyan, he still found time to campaign against window and hearth taxes. At a meeting of householders of the parish, Fyan was elected with four others to drum up support in the neighbourhood to launch an appeal to the authorities for the abolition of the taxes. Members resolved that the taxes on windows and hearths had led to a society where 'an army of beggars [were left] devouring what the army of tax-gatherers had left behind'. They complained that the window and hearth taxes, in effect, drove the infirm to their graves by placing charges on them for light and heat which they were unable to afford.[37]

In 1825 Fyan joined Daniel O'Connell in signing

a petition against the British government's attempts to suppress the Catholic Association as it continued its fight for Catholic emancipation.[38] Following the introduction of Catholic emancipation four years later, Fyan was again at the forefront of a campaign to set up a fund to pay a national tribute to O'Connell.[39]

Towards the end of his business life, Fyan continued to keep a keen eye on his commercial interests. At a meeting of grocers and other spirit dealers of Dublin in 1835, he demanded that parliament be petitioned to abolish the system of imposing excise duties on Irish whiskey, which he said was 'incompatible with justice or the fair and legitimate principles of trade'.[40] The following year he was elected chairman of the Licensed Retail Grocers and Vintners' Society.[41]

Fortune smiled on Fyan again in 1843, when Conciliation Hall was erected on Burgh Quay.[42] The building was the location of large meetings held by Daniel O'Connell to promote his campaign for the repeal of the Act of Union (1801), and of several showdowns he had with the Young Irelanders.[43] However, the boost that this gave to Fyan's trade did not tempt him to remain in business. After the death of his wife, Mary, in 1842, and with his advancing years, Fyan decided to sell up and retire to a house in Baggot Street, Dublin.[44] Dozens of items were auctioned inside and outside the Poolbeg Street premises, including two eight-day clocks, five painted window blinds, a hip bath and fifty books.[45]

Fyan's death in 1851, in his ninetieth year, marked the passing of one of Poolbeg Street's longest-living and most prominent residents, who had lived through the 1798 Rebellion, the Napoleonic Wars, the granting of Catholic emancipation and the Famine.[46] A legal document detailing his business said that Fyan had 'raised a considerable fortune on the premises', describing his enterprise as 'a well-known and long established grocery and vintner's establishment'.[47] His colourful wording of motions at meetings to demand help for the destitute or encouragement for business, along with the inscriptions he chose for his tokens, showed that he was a man not only able to coin a phrase but also phrase a coin. No doubt during his lifetime Talbot Fyan had listened to the many seafaring customers who had told him stories of their interesting and dangerous voyages. Fyan could claim to have negotiated another kind of 'seven Cs': the varied and sometimes choppy waters of campaigning, charity, child-rearing, coinage, commerce, community and criminality.

2

COUNTER ATTACK

Thomas Halpin, who operated a grocery and spirit dealership on Townsend Street, bought the premises on Poolbeg Street from Talbot Fyan in 1846 and installed Alicia Halpin to manage the business.[1] In 1851 she married John Mulligan, a twenty-six-year-old grocer from Moynalvey, County Meath, and together they began running the outlet.[2] Mulligan was one of nine children born to James and Marcella Mulligan, née Keegan, who ran a farm and kept a grocery store at Moynalvey.[3]

A year after his marriage, Mulligan attended a meeting of the Licensed Retail Grocers and Vintners' Society, and was admitted as a member. Another Poolbeg Street publican, Thomas McGrath, said that when he told Mulligan he could pay his subscription quarterly, he replied that 'the progress of the society was so satisfactory that he could not think of giving less than a year's subscription'. Another member said he 'had the pleasure of knowing Mr Mulligan to be a worthy citizen, and wished to second his admission'.[4] A week later, Mulligan became chairman of the society.[5] However, Mulligan's involvement in business campaigns, similar to Talbot Fyan's, diminished over the years, though he did subscribe ten shillings to fund an initiative to oppose the closing of licensed premises on Sundays. He also contributed to charitable causes, as Fyan had done.[6]

John and Alicia Mulligan had their first child, Mary Ann, in 1853. A son, James, followed two years later and another son, Patrick, was born in 1857. Mary Ann died when she was six years old and Patrick died two years later. The causes of their deaths were not recorded. The dangers lurking in their neighbourhood would not have eased the minds of the Mulligans when, by 1862, they were left with only one surviving child, James.

Reports of crimes in the area continued to appear in the newspapers. John Mulligan was the victim of an attack by a gang of coalmen. The origin of the dispute rested with comments Mulligan had reportedly made about the Crampton monument, which had been erected at the junction of College Street, Pearse Street and D'Olier Street in 1862. The structure, which included a fountain, was put up in honour of a former Irish surgeon general and anatomist, Sir Philip Crampton. The memorial became an immediate source of curiosity to Dubliners, who gave it several nicknames, including 'the water babe', 'the cauliflower' and 'the pineapple'. (The monument is mentioned in James Joyce's *Ulysses*, but was removed in 1959.) That Mulligan's comments about it should have been the source of such a violent assault on him, is peculiar. None of the newspaper reports of the incident gives any background to the dispute other than that it arose out of Mulligan's criticism of the monument. *The Freeman's Journal* published an account of the court proceedings in a flowery and humorous style, but this does not take away from the impact the attack would have had on John and Alicia Mulligan who, at the time, were dealing with the recent deaths of two of their three children:

> Thomas O'Keeffe, a duly qualified coal porter … was charged with having assaulted Mr John Mulligan at Poolbeg Street and also with having struck and kicked the peace officer, when taking him into captivity … On Thursday, a number of friends and promoters of fine arts assembled in Poolbeg Street for the purpose of booting [*sic*] and hallooing in the front of the shop of Mr Mulligan, who, it was generally believed by the majority of the meeting, had said something disrespectful of the Crampton monument at the end of [Pearse] Street … [O'Keeffe] said if they wanted to have the fine arts flourish they should break all Mulligan's windows and make him put in stained glass composed of old newspapers and that a deputation should wait on him to beat him … Mr Mulligan came forward to remonstrate with the meeting, when O'Keeffe proceeded to make a statue of him in a horizontal position. Mr O'Keeffe … was ordered to pay a fine of one shilling or in default to be imprisoned for one month for having assaulted Mr Mulligan.[7]

It was in this climate that John Mulligan received another blow, this time to his business. A customer, Peter Reilly, who had been drinking in Mulligan's, went home and kicked his wife, Catherine, to death. The killing attracted great attention in Ireland and was reported in the international press. For a time, it seemed that the world was focusing on John Mulligan and his shop.

This and other reports of violent incidents linked to alcohol consumption sharpened the critical focus on all licensed traders, who, throughout the 1860s, were fixed in the cross-hairs of politicians and religious leaders. The incident gave ammunition to those who believed that all sellers of alcohol should have punitive laws imposed on them, or that they should be stripped of their licences. Interest in the case increased as details of the horrendous nature of the attack were published. The case includes elements similar to those in 'Counterparts', James Joyce's short story as found in his book *Dubliners*; written some four decades later, it is partly set in Mulligan's.[8]

Peter Reilly was described as a low-sized, stout man of forty-three years of age, with nothing in his appearance to indicate ferocity or a tendency to commit an act of such terrible violence as that with which he had been charged. The inquest opened at Jervis Street Hospital on 23 January 1868. The first to give evidence was Catherine Skene, the victim's mother, who described the scene she saw when she arrived at the house:

I went to the bedroom but there was no light in the place. It was about 1 o'clock on Wednesday morning. I told Agnes to light a match, and then I saw my daughter lying on the floor in a pool of blood. She was quite naked. Her head was under the shelf of the dressing table. I went to take a quilt off the bed to cover her but Reilly would not allow me. I then took off my cloak and spread it over her. I called him either a murderer or a monster and asked him to come to an hospital in order to get some assistance. He bid me take her where I liked.

She concluded her evidence by telling the jury that she stayed with her daughter until a priest arrived and asked her to leave. Catherine Reilly died five minutes later.

The second witness to give evidence was Philip Reilly, described as 'a fine intelligent boy of about eleven years of age'. The reporter for *The Freeman's Journal* said the boy displayed great sensibility while he gave his evidence but that his father did not display any emotion. The wording and phraseology of the boy's evidence appears to have been polished for publication:

On Tuesday night last my father brought myself and my younger brother to the pantomime at the Theatre Royal.[9] When the pantomime was over we [went] to John Mulligan's public house, Poolbeg Street, where my father met a friend of his named Hughes with whom he had some drink after which the friend brought [us] home at about 11 o'clock. Hughes waited till the door was opened by my brother, Peter, who is going on 6 years of age, and then went away.

My father came in with us but afterwards went out for a short time, about three minutes. When he came in the second time my mother went to hide from him under the bed. He took off the big coat he has on him now and pulled her out by the

hair of the head and beat her about the ribs. After beating her
into a fit he desired my little brother to throw water upon her
as she lay upon the floor. After she was on the floor she never
spoke a word but was working in a fit. After the fit, Dada kicked
her [in] the back, the side and under the ribs. I saw blood on the
floor and about her dress. I saw her when [I was] in the kitchen
thrown by my father against the grate; that cut her above the
eye … I think mother had a little drink that night.

After that, he dragged her by the hair of the head into the
bedroom. I then saw him kicking her again. He then took the
candle and was going to set fire to her but her petticoats were
wet and they would not burn. He then pulled her over to the
fireplace when her clothes would not take [the fire] and laid her
back across the fender and put her head under the grate. There
was a fire burning at the time.[10]

Philip Reilly then told the jury that his younger brother,
Peter, cried in the bed and his father went to beat him. While
his father was out of the room, the boy pulled his mother
away from the fire:

After that, father kicked mother and I heard something inside
her crack … I went then for my grandmother and she came
along with my Aunt Agnes to the house.

Inspector Feeney gave evidence that when he went to the
Reilly household he found Peter Reilly's hands and the left
side of his shirt smeared with blood.

Dr Anthony Corley, who carried out a post-mortem examination on the victim, outlined the injuries she had received:

[I] found a tumour on the upper back part of the head and a contusion over the eye which was extensively blackened. The head, face and neck were all covered with scratches and contusions as were the hands and arms, both sides of the thorax and right side of the abdomen, hip, thighs and left leg ... The membrane lining the chest was lacerated into the vulva. There were extensive cuts under the scalp ... When the scalp was removed extensive effusion of blood was found ... on the abdomen was found a great effusion of blood and on the anterior region of the left kidney from rupture of that organ ... On opening the chest the fourth, fifth, eighth and tenth ribs were found each to be broken in one place and the ninth in three places.

The jury found that Catherine Reilly's death was caused by injuries inflicted on her by her husband.[11]

The case came to trial three months later, when Peter Reilly pleaded guilty to manslaughter. Reilly's employer and others gave evidence that he was a man of good character. Mr Justice O'Hagan, presiding, took an indirect swipe at John Mulligan, describing the case as one in which 'ruin and misery were brought upon individuals and families by indulgence and intoxication, a vice through which the holiest bonds that bind together human beings were wrenched asunder and misery brought upon helpless wives and innocent children'. Reilly was sentenced to serve twenty years' penal servitude.[12]

Following these tragic events, John Mulligan apparently led a quiet life, devoting his time to work and family. In 1874 he employed the services of a house painter, George Booker, to decorate areas of the premises, including the back lounge that had just been erected and is described in the contract as the 'large new room off shop'. The cost of the work was put at £14 10s., but in the contract this was altered to £13 10s., indicating that Mulligan had some skill in hammering out a bargain.[13]

A year later Mulligan died of consumption, at the age of forty-nine.[14] He left behind an estate valued a little below £6,000 – roughly equivalent to half a million pounds sterling or more than €600,000 today – and another important legacy, his name.[15] He had enough commercial sense to exploit the goodwill that Talbot Fyan had built up by placing the date of his shop's establishment in a prominent position. Today the name 'John Mulligan' is displayed outside the premises and inside along a beam in the bar, next to a shorter beam announcing 'Est. 1782'. All subsequent owners have honoured his name by retaining it, and have followed his decision to advertise the longevity of the business.

3

Counter Intelligence

The house in which James Mulligan was born, 78 Eccles Street, Dublin, was opposite one of the most famous addresses in world literature.[1] This was No. 7, the address used by James Joyce for the home of Leopold Bloom, the fictional hero of his novel *Ulysses*. The odyssey of James Mulligan's life brought a more direct connection with the author in later years, however.

As a child James Mulligan learned at first hand the misery that death could bring. When he was five his sister, Mary Ann, who was two years older than him, died. His five-year-old brother, Patrick, died when James was seven, leaving him an only child. Later, his marriage at the age of twenty to Anastasia Gray, in July 1875, would be tinged with sadness by the death of his father five months earlier.

Anastasia wasted little time in putting her stamp on her new home. She and James contracted the same painter and decorator used by John Mulligan, George Booker, to do work on areas of the building in which they lived and worked. This latest contract between the Mulligans and Booker put the cost of the work at £47, but this amount was struck out and replaced by the sum of £45.[2] John Mulligan had also been given a discount in his negotiations with Booker.

In the final months of Anastasia's first pregnancy, in 1877, James's paternal grandmother, Marcella, died, followed three weeks later by his mother, Alicia. James and Anastasia's daughter, Mary Alicia, was born on 1 June in that year.

These family tragedies gave James a greater sense of his own mortality. He had also been strengthened rather than weakened by the assault on his father by the coalman Thomas O'Keeffe, and by the reputational damage caused to the business by the Peter Reilly manslaughter case. This strength manifested itself in the exceptional steps James took to keep an orderly house. His hardiness stood him in good stead as further attacks were directed at Mulligan's from temperance campaigners. Four campaigners had recently conducted a detailed study of drinking establishments in Dublin and published their findings in *The Freeman's Journal*.[3] They opened their report by describing Dublin as a 'sink of intoxication reeking up to heaven every night'. They reserved their most pointed attack for spirit grocers, among them James Mulligan.

Another, more tangible attack on his business came from neighbours who engaged in the illicit sale of alcohol. Mary Kelly of Poolbeg Street was fined forty shillings, with the alternative of a month's imprisonment, for keeping porter without having a licence. The judge observed that Poolbeg Street was 'a warren of shebeen houses'.[4] Another local resident, Alicia Sloane, was charged with a similar offence. A policeman gave evidence that, on searching her premises, he found '103 bottles full of porter' in an ash pit at the back of her premises. The defendant denied that the porter was her property but was still fined forty shillings.[5]

A third element hampering Mulligan's business was the continuing outbreaks of riots and other crimes in the vicinity. In 1883 a newspaper advertisement offered a reward to anyone who could give 'correct information relative to the breaking of Mary McGrath's arm, 1 Poolbeg Street'.[6] Two neighbours of James Mulligan, Thomas Mitchell and his son Patrick, were brought to court on charges arising from a riot that erupted when policemen attempted to arrest Patrick Mitchell. Up to 200 people in nearby Townsend Street attacked the constables. Two policemen were injured in the disturbance; one was knocked senseless after he was hit on the head with a brick, the other was butted in the stomach and kicked in the back.[7]

Edward White, a coal porter who lived beside Mulligan's, was mentioned in a curious court case in which evidence was given that a man had thrown a woman into the Liffey at Butt bridge. A witness, Mary Brennan, ran from the scene calling for the police, but was stopped in her tracks by White, who had not been involved in the incident on the bridge. White told her that, 'Only for me and the likes of me, the country would not be in the state it is', before punching her in the face and knocking her out.[8]

Anne Colly, who lived five doors up from Mulligan's, was charged with being a dangerous lunatic and liable to commit a crime. The court heard that, after she was arrested, she was found to be carrying £760 (equivalent to about £70,000

[€81,000] today), which weighed five stone (equivalent to thirty-one kilogrammes) and had been inherited from her father. The policeman who had arrested her told the court that some of the money was in wallets suspended around her body, while more was carried in small bags tied to her clothes with strings and some of the money was sewn into her clothes. He also said it appeared that the woman had been carrying the money around for a decade and had not taken off her clothes for years:

Judge – Why did you carry all this money with you?
The accused – To save myself from being robbed.[9]

Such cases, which provided either amusement or shock to newspaper readers, showed the volatility of Poolbeg Street, where dangers or difficulties lurked in the most unlikely of people, including neighbours.

Aside from living in such a neighbourhood, James Mulligan had to deal with threats from customers who might, within a moment, become violent or rowdy. His manager, Paddy Flynn, who came from Ballyjamesduff in County Cavan, explained the device his employer used to quickly identify customers unsteady on their feet, who would then not be served: 'There wasn't a seat or stool in sight. James Mulligan couldn't abide the sight of a seat or stool. He believed you should stand up and drink your pints like a man.'[10]

Aside from fortifying his premises to counter violent or rowdy customers, James also strengthened another form of security, namely his income. He held small shareholdings in Boland's Limited and Dublin Distillers. He became one of the largest shareholders in the Hibernian Bank and was a regular contributor to debates at its annual general meetings.[11] He was also a contributor to charitable causes and institutions.[12] Despite never being in any way prominently associated with politics, he was a supporter of Charles Stewart Parnell and his party.[13]

One of James' two great hobbies was pony-trotting. He was regularly seen driving at Jones' Road, Dublin, and at other tracks. He was the owner of several trotting ponies, with which he won a number of prizes in Ireland and England.[14] James also went into partnership with his brother-in-law, John Gray, to run a sizeable farm in Staffordstown in County Meath.[15]

His second great love in life was the stage. From an early age, James became entranced by the Theatre Royal, which was situated opposite Mulligan's. As a young boy, he took breaks from collecting glasses to stand at the pub door to marvel at the comings and goings of theatregoers, before being ordered back to work by his father, but not before he had taken in the excitement outside.

In 1880 the Theatre Royal, which brought James such wonder as a curious child and such joy in adulthood as a spectator, was destroyed by fire. *The Irish Times* reported: 'Not one beam or pillar that had formed a portion of the interior of the Royal remains standing today.'[16] However, within a few years, the Leinster Hall was built on the site and attracted equally big theatrical names.[17] Dame Nellie Melba, the famous Australian operatic soprano, gave two concerts there in 1893.[18]

The Leinster Hall was converted and reopened under its previous name, the Theatre Royal Hippodrome, in 1897.[19] The same year saw the opening of another theatre, the Grand Lyric Hall (later the Tivoli Theatre), on the site of the Conciliation Hall, which had been opened by Daniel O'Connell almost sixty years earlier.[20]

The opening of Tara Street railway station on George's Quay in 1891 brought further custom to Mulligan's, as travellers who had been delayed or who had arrived too early, used the pub to while away the waiting time.[21] The extra business generated by these developments was reflected in the number of staff James employed: by 1901, two general servants and four grocery assistants.[22]

Mulligan's took on extra staff on busy days. John Joseph Kelly was one of those given occasional employment in Mulligan's during the first years of the twentieth century, when he was in his early teens. His granddaughter, Jan Kelly, said the story among her family was that he had to keep his shifts in Mulligan's secret: '[He] had been working at a grocery market but wanted to bring more money home to the family so [he] took a job at Mulligan's. One evening he was asked to deliver a tray of beers to the back/private room and served his father. They say that he didn't spill a drop. I'm not sure if he got into trouble, or how much trouble he got into!'[23]

The new Theatre Royal Hippodrome provided James

with an opportunity to combine his great passion for the stage with his canny business ventures. He had been active in its development and became a large shareholder, but his interest went further than merely attending annual general meetings. He was well acquainted with some of the greatest actors of his time:

> [James] was heart and soul taken up with the new theatre and not a day passed that did not see him at the theatre offering such assistance as he could. He had met and was on terms of friendship with Sir Henry Irving, Herbert Beerbohm Tree, Fred Terry, Julia Neilson, Ellen Terry and Sir R. [sic] Forbes Robertson.[24]

James also manned the box office every day, counted the takings and made the lodgements.[25] The comedians of the Theatre Royal often spoke of him on the stage, and he is said to have taken these quips in the best of good humour.[26]

Whatever peace and harmony existed in Poolbeg Street was threatened by the rising tension between union and non-union workers and employers, which came to a climax with the 1913 Lock-out.[27] However, labour tensions in the area had been bubbling up for more than twenty years before this. In 1891 a corn porter in Poolbeg Street had been assaulted by a fellow worker for passing a picket.[28] During the Lock-out James and his staff had to remain alert to the possibility of a fight erupting if a non-union worker arrived on the premises when several union members were drinking there.

Many non-union or 'free' labourers carried guns to protect themselves from possible attacks by strikers. In December 1913 a non-union worker from Wales, James Lewis, was driving a cartload of cement through Dublin. He had driven unmolested from the North Wall, across O'Connell Street, along Burgh Quay and through Hawkins Street before turning onto Poolbeg Street. There a man jumped onto his cart, 'presumably to pull the driver to the ground'. Six more people ran towards the cart to attack it, when Lewis pulled out a gun and fired a shot above the heads of his assailants. However, the bullet grazed the forehead of an innocent bystander, John Holloway, a shipbroker and vice-chairman of the board of Dublin Port and Docks. He was brought into Mulligan's where he was given first aid and then transferred to hospital, where he made a full recovery.[29] The Lock-out ended the following month.

At this time, another tempest, part of which involved Mulligan's name, although not the pub itself, was also blowing itself out. James Joyce's collection of short stories, *Dubliners*, had been the subject of protracted rows between the author and potential publishers, who had demanded change after change before agreeing to a contract to issue the book. The tortuous road to publication for *Dubliners* presaged Joyce's future works, *Ulysses* and *Finnegans Wake*.

One of the stories in *Dubliners*, 'Counterparts', tells of an alcoholic clerical officer called Farrington, who has a row with his employer. Farrington slips out of the office, pawns his watch and begins a pub crawl through Dublin with friends which includes Mulligan's. His mood becomes darker and darker as he suffers, among other trials, the rain, jibes from his friends and unrequited lusty glances at a beautiful woman. According to Joyce's most assiduous biographer, Richard Ellmann, 'Counterparts' was finished by 16 July 1905. It and 'The Boarding-House' are the most savage stories in *Dubliners*. Joyce, who was living in Trieste, Italy (the city was then part of the Austro-Hungarian Empire), put the mercilessness of the two stories down to the Triestine heat: 'Many of the frigidities of *The Boarding-House* and *Counterparts* were written while the sweat streamed down my face on to the handkerchief which protected my collar.'[30]

The section in 'Counterparts' dealing with Mulligan's illustrates Joyce's knowledge of the pub. Joyce lived at several addresses in Dublin but none in the vicinity of Mulligan's. However, the author frequented many pubs in the city, Mulligan's among them. While it is likely that Joyce may have been served by James Mulligan, there is no evidence to suggest that they knew each other personally. In 'Counterparts', we find that Joyce was aware that Mulligan's was a theatre pub, that performers from the nearby Tivoli Theatre drank there and, in the pub itself, the location of the snug – 'the parlour at the back'. He also knew the neighbourhood. 'Counterparts' is set, in part, in the Scotch House on Hawkins Street. In later works, Joyce also mentioned structures in the area including the Tara Street baths, the Crampton monument (both in *Ulysses*) and the Loopline bridge near Tara Street station (*Finnegans Wake*).

'Counterparts' gives expression to textual devices that Joyce would fine-tune and display to great effect in later works including his, at times, apt but curious use of phrases ('He was so angry that he lost count of the conversation of his friends'), his sharp talent for translating human gestures onto the bright screen of the reader's mind ('Farrington gazed admiringly at the plump arm which she moved very often and with much grace'), and his acute sense of accuracy and proportion in recording human expressions ('"Sh, sh!" said O'Halloran, observing the violent expression of Farrington's face.'). The humiliations Farrington suffers in the pub include one meted out by Weathers, an acrobat and knock-about artist performing at the Tivoli Theatre nearby:

When the Scotch House closed they went round to Mulligan's. They went into the parlour at the back and O'Halloran ordered small hot specials all round. They were all beginning to feel mellow. Farrington was just standing another round when Weathers came back. Much to Farrington's relief he drank a glass of bitter this time. Funds were getting low but they had enough to keep them going. Presently two young women with big hats and a young man in a check suit came in and sat at a table close by. Weathers saluted them and told the company that they were out of the Tivoli. Farrington's eyes wandered at every moment in the direction of one of the young women. There was something striking in her appearance. An immense scarf of peacock-blue muslin was wound round her hat and knotted in a great bow under her chin; and she wore bright yellow gloves, reaching to the elbow. Farrington gazed admiringly at the plump arm which she moved very often and with much grace; and when, after a little time, she answered his gaze he admired still more her large dark brown eyes. The oblique staring expression in them fascinated him. She glanced at him once or twice and, when the party was leaving the room, she brushed against his chair and said 'O, pardon!' in a London accent. He watched her leave the room in the hope that she would look back at him, but he was disappointed. He cursed his want of money and cursed all the rounds he had stood, particularly all the whiskies and Apollinaris which he had stood to Weathers. If there was one thing that he hated it was a sponge. He was so angry that he lost count of the conversation of his friends.

When Paddy Leonard called him he found that they were talking about feats of strength. Weathers was showing his biceps muscle to the company and boasting so much that the other two had called on Farrington to uphold the national honour. Farrington pulled up his sleeve accordingly and showed his biceps muscle to the company. The two arms were examined and compared and finally it was agreed to have a trial of strength. The table was cleared and the two men rested their elbows on it, clasping hands. When Paddy Leonard said 'Go!' each was to try to bring down the other's hand on to the table. Farrington looked very serious and determined.

The trial began. After about thirty seconds Weathers brought his opponent's hand slowly down on to the table. Farrington's dark wine-coloured face flushed darker still with anger and humiliation at having been defeated by such a stripling.

'You're not to put the weight of your body behind it. Play fair,' he said.

'Who's not playing fair?' said the other.

'Come on again. The two best out of three.'

The trial began again. The veins stood out on Farrington's forehead, and the pallor of Weathers' complexion changed to peony [bright pink]. Their hands and arms trembled under the stress. After a long struggle Weathers again brought his opponent's hand slowly on to the table. There was a murmur of applause from the spectators. The curate, who was standing beside the table, nodded his red head towards the victor and said with stupid familiarity: 'Ah! that's the knack!'

'What the hell do you know about it?' said Farrington fiercely, turning on the man.

'What do you put in your gab for?'

'Sh, sh!' said O'Halloran, observing the violent expression of Farrington's face. 'Pony up, boys. We'll have just one little smahan more and then we'll be off.'[31]

When Farrington returns home, one of his five children, Tom, tells him that his mother is at chapel and offers to prepare a meal for his father. Farrington unleashes all the venom that has been instilled in him during the day and that resides naturally in his spirit. He becomes incensed that the house is in darkness and blames his son for letting the fire go out. He takes a walking stick and begins whacking the child with it. Little Tom pleads for his father to stop, offering to say a Hail Mary for him. The story ends in mid-sentence, suggesting that perhaps the child has been beaten senseless, has lost consciousness and does not know what has happened. Joyce imparts this last state to the readers, leaving them, too, bereft by the nothing that follows.

The story has several common traits to the actual assault perpetrated by Peter Reilly on his wife in 1865. Both involve a man leaving Mulligan's drunk and returning home to commit a terrible assault on a family member. The theatre, the grate, the beating of a child, the nobility of the child, the darkness of the house, the description by Joyce that Farrington's wife bullies him, and the association of the real and fictional wives with religion are other lesser elements that connect the two stories of fact and fiction. There are, however, marked differences. The attack by Farrington arises from a build-up of tension throughout the day. The attack by Reilly appeared to have come from an instantaneous surfacing of anger. Reilly's wife is seen to have provoked him. No such accusation could be made against young Tom Farrington.

The assault by Reilly occurred fifteen years before Joyce was born, but the horrific nature of the story is likely to have made it a talking point in Dublin long afterwards. Although there is no proof that Joyce was influenced by the real event and, in fact, such cases were not unusual, it is worth noting because of the number of similarities between the attack by Reilly and Joyce's narrative in 'Counterparts', most notably Mulligan's.

Several stories in *Dubliners* gave publishers the jitters. Maunsel & Co. demanded alterations or deletions to the text. Legal advisers to George Roberts, who was managing director of the firm, feared that Mulligan's and the owners of other pubs mentioned would sue, and he raised these objections with Joyce. In a letter to his brother, Stanislaus, written in 1912, Joyce took up each of the points made by Roberts' solicitor:

> Public houses are mentioned in four stories out of 15. In 3 of these stories the names are fictitious. In the 4th the names are real because the persons walked from place to place. (*Counterparts*)
>
> Nothing happens in the public houses. People drink.
>
> I offered to take a car and go with Roberts, proofs in hand, to the 3 or 4 publicans really named.
>
> I said the publicans would be glad of the advertisement.
>
> I said that I would put fictitious names for the few real ones but added that by so doing the selling value in Dublin of the book would go down.[32]

A few days later, Joyce sent a postcard to Stanislaus telling of an interview he had had with Roberts during which he (Joyce) agreed to change several real names in 'Counterparts' to fictional ones. One of the alterations Joyce suggested was to rename Mulligan's as Quinlan's.[33] Despite this, agreement could not be reached. Two years later, another publisher, Grant Richards of London, published *Dubliners*, in which Mulligan's retained its place as one of the pubs featured in 'Counterparts'.

The parlour at the back, which is mentioned in the story, is where Joyce used to drink, and it later became known as 'the Joyce Room'. It is still in use and now referred to variously as the Jockeys' Room by keen horseracing fans, who used to use it as a place for deciding bets, and as the Tabernacle because of its stained-glass doors. (Joyce would use the name Mulligan prominently again for one of the main characters in his novel *Ulysses*. The book's publication in Paris in 1922 marked out Joyce as one of the most original, intriguing and influential writers in history.)

Dubliners was published when Joyce's reputation was only beginning to build. At the time its importance was not fully realised. In hindsight, some scholars regard the appearance of *Dubliners* in 1914 as a seismic event in world literature. Other events that would also have far-reaching consequences were about to occur in the fight for Irish nationhood, and here, too, Mulligan's played a small part.

The pub escaped the damage wrought elsewhere in Dublin by the 1916 Rising; it was safely tucked away from the main theatre of war at the GPO in O'Connell Street. However, in 1921, two years after the start of the War of Independence, Mulligan's was brought directly into the centre of the action. Paddy Flynn, who was then serving his time as a barman at Crilly's pub in Townsend Street, recalled the atmosphere in the city at the time:

We had the curfew then, 9 o'clock at night till 6 a.m. and if you put your nose out you'd be taking a chance; you wouldn't know when you'd be sprayed with bullets ... The Black and Tans used to come roaring down in their Crossley tenders and you'd be terrified, particularly when they'd beam in their powerful lights all over the place – you'd expect anything.[34]

Mulligan's was one of eleven buildings in Dublin raided by the British forces on 12 February 1921.[35] Despite the raid and the thoroughness of the search, nothing was found. James Mulligan had, over the years, honed his skills at averting expected and unexpected trouble. He had learned his art from dealing with riots, vandals, thieves, fires and difficult customers. A later owner of the premises, Tommie Cusack, maintained that the Black and Tans were looking for rifles but failed to find them. The story goes that they had been hidden in a place considered off-limits and even sacred, a place too conspicuous for the Black and Tans to consider. The raiders did not look inside the grandfather clock, the bottom casing of which is hollow, the pendulum taking up only about one-third of its inner casing.[36] Apart from the raid and the reported concealment of the rifles, there is nothing to suggest that James Mulligan was involved with or sympathetic towards the IRA.

Turbulence, both personal and national, continued to affect James in the 1920s. His wife, Anastasia, died in April 1921.[37] The following December the Anglo-Irish Treaty was signed in London, allowing for the establishment of the Irish Free State. Mulligan's escaped damage in the Civil War that followed between militant parties for and against the Treaty.

The publication of *Ulysses* by James Joyce in 1922 provided another link between Mulligan's and Joyce. In the novel the solicitor retained by James Mulligan, Sir George Drevar Fottrell, is mentioned twice. The Mulligan family had been employing the services of the Fottrell firm for more than half a century.[38] This connection shows that James Mulligan was familiar with the landscape of Dublin's commercial life, which James Joyce also knew, or knew of, and wrote about. Another of these connections, mentioned previously, was the house owned by James on Eccles Street which stood opposite one which Joyce used as the home for Leopold Bloom in *Ulysses*. James sold his house in 1928.[39] His decision was prompted by the death of his son-in-law, Daniel J. O'Brien, who had lived in it with his wife.[40] James's own health began to falter around this time; he was diagnosed with consumption and regularly saw his doctor, E. E. Lennon of Merrion Square, Dublin.[41]

The Theatre Royal continued to attract large crowds and boost the takings in Mulligan's. Paddy Flynn, who had been working in Mulligan's since 1925, recalled the impact of the Royal on Poolbeg Street, on Mulligan's and on James Mulligan himself:

Artistes came from all over England with their cheery ways and their cocky speech and their various revues. They were the times of the revues … The companies used to come in on Monday mornings with their lorries and they'd have their own scenery. They'd fit it up for the rehearsal and, after that, [they went] over to Mulligan's for a drink. The boss used to get a few passes for the shows and though he was a strict man there must have been a soft streak because he used to give one to me and say: 'Mind now and be home early'.[42]

The (Theatre) Royal bar stayed open for an hour after the shows, and Paddy remembers the crowds used to slink out of Mulligan's to be in their seats before the Royal door was closed. 'We never had a bit of bother clearing the house on those nights,' he said.

James died in 1931 at the age of seventy-five.[43] His dedication to his work was mentioned in an obituary in the *Irish Independent*, which observed that he had 'clung to his home to the day of his death, and the blandishments of his motoring friends could rarely if ever persuade him to forsake its locality even for a few hours'.[44] His large funeral was attended by, among others, managers of the Theatre Royal and the Gaiety Theatre, representatives of the legal profession, including the chief state solicitor, politicians and leading businessmen.

The anonymous writer of his obituary in *The Irish Times* obviously knew James well. He recalled James's interest in the old Theatre Royal (1821–80) and in the Leinster Hall, noting that James 'had many a story to tell of those old times'.[45]

In his will, James left his investments and savings to his widowed daughter, Mary Alicia, and his holding in a farm in Meath to his brother-in-law, John Gray. Another beneficiary in the will was Michael Smith, James's foreman, who was not related to him. By the time of James's death, Smith had been working in Mulligan's for a quarter of a century and had earned the respect and trust of his employer. James bequeathed the business that his father John had left to him, Mulligan's of Poolbeg Street, lock, stock and barrel to Michael Smith.

4

Press Thunders,
Stage Lights

Michael Smith inherited not only the grand old pub of Poolbeg Street from James Mulligan, but, over time, he had also acquired the skills and dedication that had characterised his former employer.[1] Smith, who was born in 1885, was a native of the townland of Crosskeys, County Cavan, situated midway between Cavan town and Ballyjamesduff. He left the family farm for Dublin in his early teenage years and worked in a pub in Parnell Street before securing employment as an assistant grocer/publican with Mulligan's.[2]

In 1925 Paddy Flynn joined Mulligan's staff. Flynn described his entry to the establishment in an interview he gave in 1983:

> 'I came from Ballyjamesduff to learn the trade. We all came, all the young fellows, it was the thing to do.' He was fifteen when he arrived to serve his time in Crilly's of Townsend Street: 'It was 1919 and, for a young fellow up from the country, it was like coming to a different world' … When Paddy Flynn had finished his time [in Crilly's] he remembers a young Australian called and he told him he was leaving Mulligan's and that if he applied he might get the job.

'I applied and I got it, and I never knew then as I was walking in that door that I would be there for a lifetime.'[3]

Kevin C. Kearns, in his book, *Dublin Pub Life and Lore – An Oral History*, observes that: 'Though most publicans were tough taskmasters, many adopted a paternal attitude towards their young wards.'[4] James Mulligan had hired Michael Smith when he was a boy, had seen him grow up and had worked with him for more than a quarter of a century. James worked every day in the Theatre Royal box office and entrusted the running of the pub to Smith during admission times. The result of this close working relationship was James Mulligan's decision to leave his business to Smith, strongly indicating that he had a fatherly attitude towards his foreman.

Having worked in the trade for thirty years, Smith was now the owner of properties that included a thriving business comprising a bar, parlour, drawing-room, dining-room, kitchen, maids' room and four bedrooms. However, he did not use his new-found status as a means of delegating work to others, particularly the grimy and labour-intensive chores generally assigned to the apprentice or porter. Smith's management ethos was that everyone contributed to doing these and other jobs. Mulligan's, similar to many other licensed premises, pasted labels on the Guinness bottles which also had the pub's name and address printed on them.

Paddy Flynn recalled the exacting chores that were carried out by Smith, himself and other staff members in Mulligan's cellar, and the restrictive rules imposed on bar workers. In the

1930s bartenders, porters and apprentices were compelled to live on the premises and respect a curfew. Smith had taken over Mulligan's when the Irish Free State was just ten years old. This decade had seen a rise in puritanical Catholic Church groups whose campaigns concerning temperance brought with them attacks on bars. Aside from this, the 1927 Intoxicating Liquor Act, introduced by the Minister for Justice, Kevin O'Higgins, forced restrictions on pub opening hours, while allowing exemptions for hoteliers and restaurateurs. Some authority figures viewed publicans as near pariahs. The government code governing national teachers – which had been in force for more than half a century – precluded a woman teacher from marrying 'the owner, part owner, or occupier of a public-house or an assistant therein or other person having an interest therein'. The code also included another restriction:

> Teachers of National Schools are not permitted to carry on or engage in any business or occupation that will impair their usefulness as teachers. They are especially forbidden to keep public-houses or houses for the sale of spirituous liquors or to live in any such house.[5]

Two months after Smith had taken over Mulligan's, the first edition of *The Irish Press* was printed. Its offices, which were on Burgh Quay and backed onto Poolbeg Street, were located on the site of the Tivoli Theatre, an area that had been occupied previously by Conciliation Hall. From its inception, the newspaper faced antagonism from certain elements of society. The publication was established by the leader of Fianna Fáil, Éamon de Valera, using funds raised in the United States during the War of Independence to finance the First Dáil. The use of the monies to finance what was a de Valera-owned company became a matter of controversy throughout, and after, its existence.

The new venture added a great deal of buzz to the vicinity and custom of Mulligan's. Paddy Clare, the *Irish Press* night reporter, described the excitement of the launch, which culminated in the pushing of the button to start the presses by Margaret Pearse, mother of Patrick and Willie Pearse, both of whom had been executed after the 1916 Rising.

The thunder of the presses could be heard in Mulligan's. The noise signalled not only the launch of a new newspaper but also the beginning of a relationship between Mulligan's and *The Irish Press* that grew in strength with each passing decade, until both were joined metaphorically at the hip, the heart and the head.

The first edition of *The Irish Press* was printed on 5 September 1931, the eve of the All-Ireland senior hurling final between Cork and Kilkenny. Before the founding of *The Irish Press*, GAA events had been given little or no coverage in national Irish newspapers. Supporters of both teams with time to spare exploited the proximity of Croke Park to Burgh Quay by flocking to the *Irish Press* building out of curiosity. Many had a drink in Mulligan's. The match was a draw. A replay the following month resulted in another draw. The championship was decided in the second replay when Cork defeated

Kilkenny by 5–8 to 3–4.[6] Before and after each replay, supporters crowded into Mulligan's, establishing its reputation as a pub where fans of sport could arrange collection of tickets, meet friends and hold post-mortem examinations on games.

Daily life in Poolbeg Street would never be the same. Dick McGrath, a member of the *Irish Press* maintenance staff, said hordes of newspaper-sellers besieged the despatch area of the building on Poolbeg Street in the early hours: 'They crowded round the building and pushed and banged doors, all trying to get on the street first with their papers.'[7]

Business prospects for Smith were looking up as the circulation of *The Irish Press* rose to 100,000 copies daily. Steady custom from its staff increased profits. Mulligan's became a handy venue for journalists to conduct interviews. This extra trade cushioned Mulligan's against the effects of the economic war between Ireland and Britain that broke out in 1932, shortly after de Valera became President of the Executive Council (prime minister), and lasted for six years.[8]

The 1930s were not without their difficulties for Mulligan's, though. The launch of *The Irish Press* was followed three years later by the closure of the Theatre Royal, on which Mulligan's relied for a great part of its business. New owners decided on the closure, in part, to replace it with another on the site that would continue to stage live performances but would be more suitable to cinema audiences than the old theatre had been.[9] The curtain came down for the last time on 3 March 1934, by which time reports were already circulating that a new theatre would be erected on the site.[10]

In the meantime, Mulligan's had to make do with its local trade and the valuable custom from *The Irish Press*. In 1934 the pub got its first mention in the paper's news pages, arising from the arrival of an unlikely visitor in the bar:

> A carrier pigeon bearing the number RF264 HB LLRO flew into the rear of Mr J. Mulligan's licensed premises, Poolbeg Street, Dublin, through one of the windows.
>
> The bird showed unusual tameness, by alighting on the hand of one of the assistants who offered it some seed.[11]

The victory of Cavan over Kildare in the 1935 senior All-Ireland Gaelic football championship helped to spread the word in Cavan, the native county of Michael Smith and Paddy Flynn, that its supporters had another base in the capital which they could regard as 'a home away from home'.[12] At that time, the trade in Dublin was dominated by Cavan, Limerick and Tipperary publicans.[13]

A day after the All-Ireland, there was another sign of good fortune for Mulligan's. On 23 September 1935 the new Theatre Royal was formally opened with a concert that included a performance by Count John McCormack. The enormous building could accommodate almost 4,000 people, including standing room. It comprised bars, a cinema, a restaurant and a theatre. The new building retained the stage door entrance on Poolbeg Street opposite Mulligan's, which remained 'the local for all the performers at the Royal'.[14] Despite the sale of alcohol in the theatre, Mulligan's still benefited from the overflow during intervals and from the trade generated by patrons on their way to, or coming from, the theatre.

Mulligan's eventually found it difficult to accommodate the overspill from the Theatre Royal, and so Michael Smith decided to open up No. 9 to the public. The front section of the ground floor of No. 9 had sometimes been used as a storeroom and at other times was let out to business tenants. The back section had been used as a sitting room. Both areas were now renovated. An art deco-type wooden panel, with four parallel grooves running across it, was erected, circling the entire front lounge at a little above head height. This reflected the art deco style of the Theatre Royal. Eight Theatre Royal programmes, dating from the late nineteenth and early twentieth centuries and printed on silk, were placed behind a glass panel on the wall above the counter in the front lounge and are still there today. The large room at the rear, which was eventually to become the back lounge, was also opened to the public. Sketches from Shakespeare's plays were hung on the walls.

The outbreak of the Second World War and the prospect of an economic downturn did not dissuade Smith from going ahead with the extension. Less than two weeks after the war began, Smith applied for a certificate to enable him to receive an excise licence for the sale of alcohol at Nos 8 and 9 Poolbeg Street.[15] One of the first to record the change was the writer Flann O'Brien:

Mulligan's in the narrow street which runs alongside the Theatre Royal caters for painted ladies and painted men – the theatrical kind – often straight from the stage. Most people connected with show business make their way here, and Mr Mulligan [*sic*] has recently provided a new lounge for their entertainment and approval.[16]

The start of the war brought with it the threat of a severe depletion in Mulligan's trade because of travel restrictions that impeded British acts from travelling to Ireland to perform at the Theatre Royal and other venues. However, Louis Elliman, who owned the Theatre Royal and the Gaiety Theatre, was an astute businessman. The theatrical historian Philip B. Ryan said the period of the Second World War was Elliman's most inspired and he 'kept both the Royal and the Gaiety open with entirely Irish talent'.[17] These Irish performers included Jack Cruise, Peggy Dell, Maureen Potter, Noel Purcell and Cecil Sheridan.

On 1 September 1944 Tommie Cusack, from Lower Lavey in County Cavan, began working for his uncle, Michael Smith, in Mulligan's. He was sixteen years old. His father, who had brought him to Dublin on the weekend of the All-Ireland hurling final, called in to Mulligan's and asked Smith: 'Can you do anything with this lad?'[18] The boy began work immediately and later recalled the tasks he undertook:

It was hard work in those days but good. Five shillings a week, live in and working from ten to ten at night. Your trousers would be able to stand up straight on their own at the end of the day because you'd have to bottle the beer yourself, and the spillage was something.[19]

In 1945 James and Anastasia Mulligan's daughter Mary, the last direct link with the family, died at the age of sixty-five. She was described as 'the loveliest and warmest of people, forever up for fun who liked a game of cards'. She was very much the society woman, driving a car, resplendent in furs and wearing pearls. This all went towards complementing her lively personality, which embraced a powerful generosity of spirit. In her will, Mary, known also as May and Annie, left a solid silver tea set to her god-child, Mary O'Neill. However, it was no ordinary tea set. Mary O'Neill's mother, Kitty, told her it had been used to serve afternoon tea to Queen Victoria during her visit to Ireland in 1900. It is fitting that one of the last gestures from the Mulligan family, which had been associated so long and closely with the Theatre Royal, should involve a theatrical woman and a royal personage.[20]

Mulligan's had battled through very difficult years. It had not only survived these, but had enhanced its reputation and consequently its business. It also became the scene for a peculiarly Irish coming-of-age ceremony, described by one local as being 'Mulliganointed'. One example of this, which occurred in 1947, was documented by the former RTÉ rugby commentator Fred Cogley, whose father, Mitchel, was a staff member of *The Irish Press* before being appointed sports editor of the *Irish Independent*. Fred Cogley described his

'Mulliganointing' in an interview on the *Gay Byrne Show* on RTÉ Radio, which was reported in *The Irish Press*:

> There had been one occasion, [Fred] admitted, when alcohol passed his lips. He was aged twelve, he recalled, and in Mulligan's pub with his Da, when the latter, as fathers often will, enquired if young Fred would like to taste the head of his pint of Guinness. Fred said he would – and then proceeded to drain almost the entire glass while his father was momentarily distracted.
>
> So much for the theory of the acquired taste, as Gay observed, but though he clearly enjoyed the experience, Fred Cogley subsequently took the pledge and never touched a drop again in his life.[21]

5

AFTER THE RAINBOW, BEFORE CAMELOT

When the *Irish Press* news editor, Jack Grealish, returned home to his wife, Nora, on a September night in 1947, he told her he had met a man who, in his opinion, would become president of the United States.[1] The man he was speaking about was John F. Kennedy. The meeting, which took place in Mulligan's fourteen years before Kennedy entered the White House, is interesting not only because of the presence of the future US president, but also because of a connection he shared with Grealish.

Grealish and Kennedy had much in common.[2] Kennedy worked as a journalist for Hearst Newspapers and wrote about Ireland during a visit in 1945. As a congressman and member of an influential Boston-Irish family, Kennedy was on familiar terms with people of high standing in US politics and society. Grealish, in his career as a journalist, was well acquainted with powerful individuals in Ireland, including Éamon de Valera, the Roman Catholic Archbishop of Dublin, Dr John Charles McQuaid, and Flann O'Brien. Grealish and Kennedy also shared an interest in economics. Aside from his talents as a news editor, Grealish was highly regarded for his business acumen.

The two men also had an interest in the most effective presentation of thought and ideas through language. In 1947 Kennedy, who was thirty years old and in his first year as a member of the US House of Representatives, was at an early stage of honing the rhetorical skills that later became one of his hallmarks. Grealish, on the other hand, had worked at the challenge of making the English language sing every day of his working life.

Three years earlier Grealish had written a two-page article on Irish neutrality for *The Sign*.[3] One of his sons, Anthony, believes that this article is likely to have been the reason why Kennedy sought out his father. During his 1947 visit to Ireland, Kennedy called at the offices of *The Irish Press* on Burgh Quay. Grealish did not have much money on him and had to borrow two shillings and six pence from a colleague to take the future president of the United States to Mulligan's for a drink.

Paddy Flynn remembered that Kennedy drank a bottle of lager. He was told that Kennedy was a newspaper man and had just been honourably discharged from the US navy.[4] Kennedy, who had read James Joyce's works and was an admirer of the writer, knew of the connection between Mulligan's and the short story 'Counterparts'.[5]

Grealish, too, was an admirer of Joyce. He was well-versed in the subtleties and sounds of *Finnegans Wake* and used to explain elements of the story to his children. He had, however, a stronger connection with Joyce than Kennedy might have expected. Born in Galway city in 1910, Grealish was friendly with the family of Nora Barnacle, Joyce's wife. He also worked with her sister, Kathleen, on the *Connacht Tribune*.[6] Leaving Galway in 1931 to join *The Irish Press*, he corresponded with Nora's mother, Annie, for several years. Grealish knew very well the streets and environment of the Barnacle family, which Joyce had visited with Nora. Like many of his generation, Jack Grealish did not speak much at home about his work and life outside the family, so the elements of the conversation between him and Kennedy are lost.

The similarities between the two Jacks, such as their common interests, are unsurprising. Grealish's connection with Joyce was a happy circumstance for Kennedy to come across. The meeting was recorded briefly in a special edition of *Look* magazine following the assassination of Kennedy on 22 November 1963. The date is the source of a small coincidence involving the two men. One of the earliest photographs of Jack Grealish was taken as he posed with the rest of the staff of the *Connacht Tribune* on 22 November 1930.

Mulligan's would not benefit from the custom generated by Kennedy's visit until after he had taken office as US president in 1961. However, in the 1940s and early 1950s three institutions – *The Irish Press*, the Theatre Royal and the GAA – helped to keep the tills ringing and to further shape the culture of Mulligan's.

Indeed, Mulligan's became as much a printers' pub as one for journalists. Both were colourful ingredients in the mix of the clientèle. Michael O'Toole, who joined *The Irish Press* in 1964, recounted a confrontation between Maurice Liston[7] and the *Irish Press*'s managing editor, William J. Redmond (WJR), concerning a fire in a Dublin convent during the 1940s:

> WJR was then at the height of his powers as a disciplinarian and, as they were both departing to their separate pubs for a nightcap, he ordered Maurice to get a taxi and follow the [fire] brigade. Half an hour later, WJR left the Scotch House for Mulligan's where he found Maurice propped up at the counter with 'a formidable drink'. 'Mr Liston,' he demanded (WJR was always formal in confrontation), 'what about the fire in the Dominican convent?' Maurice was unruffled. 'I was speaking to the reverend mother,' he said, 'and she told me personally that there was f**k all in it.'[8]

The hard man's attitude and colourful language remain features of Dublin pubs. During and after the post-war years, Irish public houses were seen as 'the last bastion of male supremacy'.[9] Seán O'Donohoe, a native of County Wexford who settled in Dublin in 1943 and who worked in Mulligan's from 1951 to 1963, described the culture of segregation that existed at the time:

> When I came to Dublin in the 1940s women didn't come into pubs. If you were going with a girl you brought her to the pictures and we'd have a bag of sweets. Young girls didn't drink at that time. The old women would come in with a jug under

their shawl and they'd want a GP, which was a glass of porter, and that was four pence and you'd give it to them and you'd give them a tilly [a bonus measure] and they'd put it under their shawl and walk out. They could be dealers and then some of them would go to the wash-house and they'd do the washing in Tara Street baths at that time. Women would do the washing for people and they'd come into Mulligan's and have a drink; lovely old women.[10]

One woman who was not served in Mulligan's was Woodbine Annie, who worked as a prostitute in Poolbeg Street and whose usual charge for her services was five Woodbine cigarettes.[11]

It would be at least two decades before the campaign for women's liberation in Ireland began to make headway. Much of this future change was brought on by the women's liberation campaign, some of whose strategies were formulated in Mulligan's.

The launches of *The Sunday Press* in 1949 and the *Evening Press* in 1954 brought with them an extension of the number of journalists, printers and office staff to the Mulligan's clientèle. The Theatre Royal also continued to attract world-famous performers. Stewart Granger attended the Irish première of the film *Captain Boycott* there on 13 September 1947. Three years later the organist, Tommy Dando, began a long association with the Royal. He became famous for inviting audiences to 'Keep your sunny side up' as he and his instrument rose through an expansive trapdoor to the left of the orchestra pit.

Tommie Cusack's brother, Con, began working in Mulligan's in 1950, when the Theatre Royal was at the peak of its success.[12] Seán O'Donohoe joined the staff the following year, having been headhunted by Paddy Flynn.[13] One of the first big names he met was Eamonn Andrews, who married Grace Bourke in 1951: 'He brought all the [wedding] crowd from the Royal in to Mulligan's and I served them all. And when he was paying me out, he handed me two half crowns for a tip. That was a lot that time [sic].'[14]

However, it was the arrival of Judy Garland with her then husband Sid Luft, in late June 1951, that created the most excitement in Poolbeg Street for many years. She did fourteen shows at the Theatre Royal during the first week of July. She found that the windows of her dressing room opened out onto Poolbeg Street, facing Mulligan's, where hundreds of fans who could not get a ticket congregated: '[Each] night, before and after her show, when she returned to the dressing room, she threw open the windows and sang for them, and they serenaded her in return.'[15] Garland also went in to Mulligan's every night, bringing with her the stagehands for whom she bought drinks. She smoked and played poker in the pub seven nights running.[16]

Seán O'Donohoe enjoyed the cosmopolitan nature of the pub and its vicinity. Through the good offices of the Theatre Royal doorman, Tommy Wilkinson, Seán was allowed in to see Danny Kaye, who signed an autograph for him. In 1954, when Nat King Cole performed four shows at the Theatre Royal, he accepted another engagement at the Banba bookstore on Tara Street, an event that drew hundreds of people. As Seán recalled:

> There were crowds in Tara Street but there was no one in Poolbeg Street. We knew he was coming to do it and as Con [Cusack] and I were outside [Mulligan's] having a smoke, who walks up Poolbeg Street only Nat King Cole on his own. Not a sinner around. They thought he'd come the other way, you see. He shook hands with the two of us and spoke for a few minutes. He didn't go in for a pint and I didn't get his autograph. I enjoyed that because I love him singing [sic].[17]

The association between Mulligan's and the Theatre Royal was not confined to serving alcohol. When Joe Loss and his orchestra made their annual visits to Dublin to play the Theatre Royal, some of the musicians were put up in Poolbeg Street by Paddy Flynn.[18]

The Dublin historian, Éamonn MacThomáis, compared the running 'between the Royal queue, the Royal stage door and Mulligan's' to a mini-Olympics.[19] MacThomáis appears to suggest that people left the queue for the theatre to have a quick drink in Mulligan's while someone held their place for them. He also refers to the audience traffic, during intervals, between the theatre and Mulligan's. Indeed, during one interval, one of the resident musicians, Tommy King, ran across to Mulligan's for refreshment. On his quick return to the Royal, he fell through the open cellar hatch just outside the pub.[20]

Michael Smith's first cousin, once removed, Micheál Smyth, recalled that the Irish performers Danny Cummins, Peggy Dell, Jimmy O'Dea, Maureen Potter and Noel Purcell considered Mulligan's to be their second home. Many met in the pub on Monday nights, particularly during Lent. Smyth described his relative as a philanthropist, who looked after the poor and needy, including many acquaintances and friends of the performers.[21]

Micheál Smyth always looked forward to going to Mulligan's as a boy. The number of visits increased with the success of the Cavan football team, which won All-Irelands in 1947 (this game was played in New York), 1948 and 1952:[22]

He [Michael Smith] was so welcoming and decent it is just incredible to even think that such a man ever existed. When Cavan were going well in the late 1940s and early 1950s, we would call when in Dublin. The first thing [Smith] did was dive to the till and pluck out a ten shilling note for me. I was only five or six at the time but still remember those visits and his extreme generosity.[23]

One of the most interesting characters to frequent Mulligan's at that time was the columnist and author Flann O'Brien. While the Scotch House on the corner of Hawkins Street and Burgh Quay was his favourite haunt or, as he used to call it, his 'office', Mulligan's was one of two dozen or so pubs in which he drank. He cited the pub in his *Cruiskeen Lawn* column (written under the pseudonym, Myles na Gopaleen in *The Irish Times*) as a geographical reference point for the Theatre Royal: 'It's near two places – Phil O'Reilly's of Hawkins Street and Mulligan's of Poolbeg Street.'[24]

O'Brien's preferred tipple was a ten-year-old Jameson whiskey. He used to demand of the bartenders in Mulligan's not to pour it from the bottle they used for the customers; he would say, 'Give it to me from the parish priest's bottle.'[25] He was keenly aware of the number of journalists who drank in the pub, and maintained that 'any piece of *Irish Press* copy which didn't bear the imprint of the bottom of a porter glass from Mulligan's or the White Horse would automatically be held suspect and spiked by the chief-sub'.[26]

Soon after starting work as a barman in Mulligan's in 1951, Seán O'Donohoe became aware of the pub's ethos, that of no singing and keeping customers in order, which squared with his own. The boxer, Jack Doyle, was a regular drinker on his visits to Dublin. In his prime, Doyle had gone several rounds against formidable opponents. However, he did not get beyond the first round when he produced a forged £100 note in Mulligan's. Seán O'Donohoe refused to accept it. Other customers also proved tricky, including the musical director in the Theatre Royal, Jimmy Campbell:

> They'd all come over for a drink during the break and Jimmy would come in and he'd say: 'Seán, I forgot me wallet,' and I'd say, 'Well, Jimmy, you'd better go back for it', because he wouldn't pay you. Oh, he was a terrible man that way. He was a nice fellow, though.[27]

He remembered the poet Patrick Kavanagh coming on rare occasions to the pub and said he was always well-behaved, a sentiment that would not be echoed by many other barmen in Dublin at the time. Kavanagh was aware of the zero tolerance of bad behaviour in Mulligan's. Seán O'Donohoe recalled, however, that Brendan Behan was either not aware of it, or was and did not care:

> I had the pleasure of barring him. I wasn't on his Christmas card list and he certainly wasn't on mine. It was all dirty language, terrible. I remember [pianist and singer] Peggy Dell and [actress] Pauline Forbes [were in the pub]. They were famous and he was effing and blinding all around and I told him off. He called for a second drink and I wouldn't serve him. I never served him after. He effed me from a height. I didn't mind that. He'd come in with Benedict Kiely, but Benedict was a gentleman you know, a lovely gentleman.[28]

O'Donohoe also recalled some of the many customers who distinguished themselves by their courtesy, such as the actor Cyril Cusack, his wife, Maureen, and his family, who visited Mulligan's after attending or appearing in plays at the Abbey Theatre. Comedian Danny Cummins was also a regular. The sports commentator Micheál O'Hehir used to check the day's card with friends in the back lounge before heading off to the racecourse. Seán was friendly with the tenor, and Mulligan's regular, Josef Locke. Having bought the Listowel Arms Hotel in County Kerry, Locke offered Seán the job of running it: 'I wouldn't go. He could be troublesome.'[29]

Con Cusack described Michael Smith as a quiet, un-assuming man with a winning smile. Seán O'Donohoe remembered him as a 'real gentleman' and 'a man you could work forever with'.[30] However, customers who became rau-cous found themselves outside on the street within seconds. Bad language to Michael Smith was, according to Con Cusack, like a red rag to a bull. The power and force with which Smith ejected difficult customers were all the more surprising because of his quiet nature.

The Cusack brothers and the rest of the Mulligan's staff saw yet another side to Smith in how he dealt with robbers who had broken into a premises in Talbot Place on the north side of the Liffey. Having escaped with £535 in cash, the thieves made their way to the south side of the city, to Mulligan's, to celebrate. One of the thieves used an Irish currency £100 note to pay for three drinks. Michael Smith became suspicious and refused to change it. They were rumbled. The thieves ended up in court where one of them was sent to jail for a year.[31]

Con and Tommie Cusack soon settled into the ways of Mulligan's, becoming part of a new family, establishing a particular rapport with Paddy Flynn. The staff were left to their own devices on Sundays, when Michael Smith would make his one weekly trip out of the vicinity. He did not drive a car but kept one. His nephew, Jack, who was a mechanic at McCairns Motors, Poolbeg Street, drove Smith and Smith's aunt, Teresa, on outings to County Wicklow or to other destinations, where they would dine out.[32] These outings were not without their problems. In Michael Smith's will (schedule of assets), McCairns Motors is listed as being owed £25 and 12 shillings for 'repairs to motor car'. In the inventory of effects detailed in the will, the car, a 1961 model Vauxhall Victor, is valued at £450 and described thus: 'It is evident that this car has been involved in four or five accidents.'[33]

The Theatre Royal was a source of amazement to the Cusack brothers and to the other members of Mulligan's staff. Inside the pub there was a constant ebb and flow of theatregoers and performers. Paddy Flynn recalled the stars who frequented Mulligan's:

We got them all – Jimmy O'Dea, Jack Cruise, Jimmy Campbell, Norman Metcalfe, all the stars of those days. I think they felt if it wasn't in Mulligan's, it wasn't a drink at all.[34]

Another source of amazement was the Royalettes, a troupe of eighteen dancing women. William 'Spud' Murphy, who has been a Mulligan's regular since 1957 – longer than any other – said the first time he saw the Royalettes was the first time he had ever seen a miniskirt. A Dublin street character of the time, Bang Bang, was tolerated in Mulligan's and even engaged in mock shoot-outs with the Royalettes.[35] While it was a general rule in Dublin that women were either not welcome or not allowed into pubs, Mulligan's opened its doors to them and even reserved the Joyce Room for them at the back of the bar (No. 8) on performance nights.[36]

The Theatre Royal was growing in strength, with a

successful twenty-first anniversary show in September 1956 and performances by Liberace the following month. Then, just as Con and Tommie Cusack were getting used to the intermittent glamour of the area, a riot erupted on Poolbeg Street. The disturbances on the night of 28 February 1957 were reported on by the international and domestic media, including *The Irish Press*:

> Crowds – mostly of teenage boys and girls – began to collect in the streets around Dublin's Theatre Royal before 8 o'clock last night, the second night of the visit of the rock 'n' roll 'King' Bill Haley and his Comets at the Royal. A great cheer went up when Haley appeared at the window and waved to the crowd. After a few moments he withdrew and the gardaí began to move the fans back into Hawkins Street and Tara Street. Before they had cleared [Poolbeg Street] Haley again appeared at the window and the crowds rushed back. There were scuffles between gardaí and youths. Hundreds of youths and girls came back into [Poolbeg Street] and, for thirty minutes, they danced, shouted and sang rock 'n' roll songs. There were several fights in the crowd as people were pushed about.[37]

The riots and baton charges that ensued between the police and concertgoers in Poolbeg Street attracted worldwide attention. Con and Tommie Cusack did not know it then, but they had witnessed a historic moment – the arrival of rock and roll in Ireland.

This event was followed by the beginning of an economic boom for Mulligan's. Figures from the first three years of the

1960s show that the pub was exploiting to great effect its goodwill and the valuable custom nearby. The pub's turnover in 1960 was £20,566, with a gross profit recorded as £6,040. The following two years saw further rises: 1961, £26,678 (turnover), £8,273 (gross profit); 1962, £30,576 (turnover), £9,769 (gross profit). (The equivalent of £9,769 in today's money would be about £150,000/€180,000.) In three years, Mulligan's had increased both its turnover and gross profit by 50 per cent.

The high revenues were partly the result of custom generated by the Theatre Royal and the *Irish Press* group of workers, and partly because of the dedication of Smith and his staff to their trade. The work ethic of Tommy McDonald, who joined Mulligan's around 1960, was second to none. He soon became the colleague on whom all the others relied. He stepped in to fill shifts when other staff took holidays. He opened and closed the premises, did the orders, oversaw the exacting work of deliveries and deposited the takings in the boot of his car, which he took to the bank for lodgement. At closing time he gave lifts to other staff or customers who faced long journeys home. He managed to discharge these normal and extra duties with a quiet dignity, enthusiasm and efficiency that quickly won him the respect of his peers in Mulligan's and of others working in the trade in Dublin.[38]

Michael Smith had steered the business to a point where it enjoyed great success. He died on 24 April 1962 at the age of seventy-seven. His relative, Micheál Smyth, said Smith typified all that was good, decent and worthwhile in life. Many of the Theatre Royal performers attended his funeral mass at the Church of the Immaculate Heart of Mary, City Quay, Dublin, and travelled to the burial at Crosskeys Cemetery in County Cavan, where Noel Purcell gave the oration.[39]

6

BAR CHANGE

The beneficiaries named in Michael Smith's will ran to more than two dozen. Relatives, bar staff, his housekeeper and even his executors were among those left considerable sums of money. However, a problem arose in the manner in which the premises of Nos 8, 9 and 10 Poolbeg Street were bequeathed.

Smith ordered that a limited company be set up to run the business, and that seven directors be appointed, including Paddy Flynn, and Con and Tommie Cusack. The remaining four directors were a relative of Smith's, who was to be allowed to live over the premises, and the three executors of the will: Smith's cousin, who was also called Michael Smith, Gerard Sweetman, TD and solicitor, and John Clarke, a peace commissioner. The will ran to nine pages, detailing the formation of the company, its articles of association and what was to be done in the event of the death of one of the directors.[1] However, the interests and demands of the disparate parties ranged from remote to direct. Disagreements that emerged between them dragged on for six years before a resolution was eventually found.

In the meantime, the Cusacks and Paddy Flynn faced a more serious threat: the closure of the Theatre Royal. Rumours about its demise had been circulating for months, although Dubliners did not believe that their most treasured Royal would ever close. Despite this, the closure was confirmed by the announcement of the Royal Finale for 30 June 1962. The theatre historian Philip B. Ryan said the closure resulted from an accumulation of many factors, including the high fees demanded by visiting acts, rising overheads, the coming of television and a five-week strike in 1961 that made inroads into the theatre's reserves and appeared to dent the management's enthusiasm for continuing to run the establishment.[2]

The bulldozers moved in on the Monday following the Saturday night finale, and began to demolish the theatre. The staff and regulars of Mulligan's were surprised to see one of the Royal's stalwarts, Mickser Reid, continue to use the pub as his local. However, he was not wearing a costume such as the one he might have used in *Snow White and the Seven Dwarfs*. Instead he was in builder's clothes, as he was employed on the site as the 'tea boy'. The change from actor to gofer was difficult enough for this much-loved and talented comedian. However, he now faced yet another challenge:

He was the butt of cruel jokes about his size, but the site foreman got to hear about this and remonstrated with his men, and instructed that Mickser must be left in peace and respected like any other worker on the site. He took Mickser aside and informed him of developments, assuring him that the lads had just been having a bit of fun and really meant him no harm.

Mickser listened carefully with his Woodbine in the corner of his mouth and assured the foreman that he was accustomed to being laughed at, although he had previously been paid for it, but they were decent lads, and he understood. Just as the foreman was about to leave, Mickser added: 'Tell them it's OK and in future I'll stop pissing in the tea.'[3]

The destruction of the Theatre Royal was part of a general change that involved knocking down and rebuilding in the rush for economic expansion in Ireland in the early 1960s. The building that replaced the theatre accommodated the offices of the Department of Health, Hawkins House, described as 'the most monstrous heap of architectural scrap built in Dublin in the past twenty-five years and its sheer awfulness led to a re-assessment of the whole idea of having high buildings in the city centre'.[4] (In 1998 the building was voted the worst in Dublin by readers of *archiseek*, an online magazine dedicated, but not exclusively, to Irish architecture.[5]) Paddy Flynn recalled that the old sounds from the Theatre Royal of vans unloading sets gave way to different sounds of demolition trucks as developers moved into the area.

In 1963 Flynn turned his attention further afield, with the announcement that President John F. Kennedy was to visit Ireland. Flynn remembered Kennedy's 1947 visit to Mulligan's: 'I wrote to the American ambassador asking him could the President call in again and see us all. I got a lovely reply telling me he wouldn't have the time. Maybe in the future.'[6] Flynn also spoke to *The Irish Times* about Kennedy's forthcoming visit:

> If we knew that he was going to be the great J. F. Kennedy we would have taken down every word about him … Of course we would be delighted to see him again. But I am afraid that it would not be possible for him to call. Anyway, it would be hard for us to accommodate all the security men who are coming with him.[7]

Five months later, Seán Carberry, a journalist with *The Sunday Press*, was marking his departure from the newspaper to the *RTÉ Guide* at a party in Mulligan's:

> The hooley was still in its first hour, with the legendary Niall Carroll, political reporter and amanuensis of de Valera, rendering *Skibbereen* to 50 or so of his colleagues, when … the door burst open and a colleague roared at us, 'John F. Kennedy's been shot in Dallas'. It was, of course, November 22 1963.
>
> In all my years, before or since, I have never seen so many journalists exit a pub so fast.[8]

Jimmy Walsh, a journalist with the *Evening Press*, was returning from a tea-break at around half past six when the first reports were coming through:

> We then had about half an hour where, I suppose, the nation and much of the world was hoping against hope that things

wouldn't be as bad as they turned out to be but by 7 o'clock it was confirmed ... You can imagine, people were gravitating into the newsroom from all corners and somebody said: 'Let's do a special *Evening Press.*' They certainly had an edition on the streets by 8 o'clock. It was possibly one of the first if not *the* first newspaper in the world on the streets with the news of the assassination.[9]

The Kennedy–Mulligan's association is marked by a framed black-and-white photograph of Kennedy on the wall at the back of the bar commemorating his visit to the pub in 1947. Exactly one year after the assassination, on 22 November 1964, Tommie Cusack and his wife, Evelyn, celebrated the birth of their son, Ger (Gerald).

In the 1960s the Mulligan's name began making its presence felt in areas other than cursory mentions in domestic newspapers. Since the publication of Joyce's *Dubliners* in 1914, the pub had received scant attention in literary works, though brief reference was made to it in a short story by Benedict Kiely, published in *The Bell* in 1952.[10] Then Mulligan's was chosen by the producers of Ireland's first television soap opera, *Tolka Row*, as the basis for a pub design that was to be used as one of the sets for the RTÉ programme. The series, which first went on air in January 1964, ended in March 1968.

In 1967 the *Blade* newspaper, of Toledo, Ohio, described Mulligan's as 'the most colourful spa of all' in an article headed 'Touring Brendan Behan's Dublin':

[Mulligan's] first opened its saloon doors in 1782 and hardly looks as if it has been redecorated since. For any visitor in search of a whiff of instant Dublin, Mulligan's is the place – down by the docks, near the River Liffey, smoky and noisy, and more often than not inhabited by a hawker carrying a basket of oysters and Dublin prawns. 'They're all alive, they're all alive,' he says.[11]

During the 1960s Con and Tommie Cusack, along with Paddy Flynn, were also attempting to gain control of the business from the other beneficiaries named in Michael Smith's will, but with little success. The conclusion to the six-year dispute over the ownership of Mulligan's came in 1968. The pub was advertised for sale in national newspapers. The auctioneers did not allow the closure of the Theatre Royal to get in the way of describing the pub as having a valuable trading position surrounded by large office blocks including Hawkins House, O'Connell Bridge House, Liberty Hall and Tara House (Heiton McFerran).[12]

The pub was sold at auction on 21 March 1968 for £26,500. Under the deal, Smith's relative, who had been living upstairs in No. 8, vacated the premises. Ownership of the business came into the hands of three of the beneficiaries. *The Irish Press* reported that the pub was bought 'secretly' by Con and Tommie Cusack and Paddy Flynn. In the same report, Flynn described how the pub would be managed: 'There will be no change in the old place – we're going to preserve its character. There are too many plush pubs springing up in

Dublin. People are looking for a real man's pub where they can spit on the floor.'[13] The Cusacks and Flynn formed a company with all three holding equal shares.[14] The firm of solicitors retained by them was George D. Fottrell & Sons, the same firm that had been used by the owners of Mulligan's for the previous 113 years.

Paddy Madden, a journalist with the *Evening Press*, decided to set down his recollections of a day in the life of Mulligan's from around that time. This one-off diary, written in 1996, was presented to the pub owners as a souvenir. The record offers another connection between Mulligan's and John F. Kennedy. The day Madden chose to set his piece was the day of the assassination of John F. Kennedy's brother, Robert, in Los Angeles on 6 June 1968:

MULLIGAN'S

One day in the lovely Summer of 1968.

Poolbeg Street in downtown Dublin on a glorious morning in 1968. It's shortly after 10.45 a.m. and, as the doors of Mulligan's swing open, the world of commerce tip-toes unsteadily forward to renew its ancient joust with the world of alcohol in the Cusack emporium.

10.55: already the lounge is buzzing along nicely. Jockser, we never knew his real name, is wrapped around his first pint of the day and Butterkrust [Mick Byrne] is chaining his Rudge bike to a car outside the leather shop.[15]

The conversation at the bar is much the same as a thousand yesterdays – the lousy state of the government, the loud mouths from Trinity who blighted the pub the previous evening and, of course, the price of the pint. Yes, indeed, the ultimate coalition of democracy and academia – a people's parliament where ordinary folk have their say and where Tommie Cusack, in the role of Speaker of the House, presides ever so eloquently – on a sun-filled June morning is as sharp and as loquacious as any university in God's world.

11.15: the giant presses in the newspaper next door are growling. Butterkrust, Jockser and other parliamentarians check the clock above the bar wall and mutter their expected dog-eared comments. 'Jaysus, they're a bit late today.' Precisely fifteen seconds later the stool under the picture from the Theatre Royal is occupied by another thespian of sorts. The smallish rotund man is Paddy Flynn, sports editor of the *Evening Press*, reporting for real duty: Minister for Sport, Opposition spokesman for just about everything. The man from Longford with a thousand answers, a thousand questions, a thousand put-downs. A man for all Mulligan's mornings. But, for the ordinary punter in this extraordinary bar he's a man you'd cross a thousand bridges to meet … and to bask in his beautiful, yet totally irreverent, shadow.

On that June morning twenty-eight years ago, I was not only the most junior of juniors in Paddy Flynn's sports department, but also the lowest form of human life in Mull's as well.

My job description in the Cusack shop – Dublin term for pub – was a mixture of Victorian chimney boy, supplier of papers for Paddy's cronies and, most important of all – organiser of emergency cash for the boss when the going got lean. The call always came in the mid-afternoon. 'Bring me my coat, twelve

Evening Presses and two quid. Where you get the money is your business, just get in here quickly.'

11.35: appalling news from the crackling wire service machine in the newsroom of the *Evening Press* is quickly transferred to the branch office thirty paces away; a crazed Palestinian has pumped five bullets into the head of Bobby Kennedy in the Ambassador Hotel in Los Angeles. Sirhan Sirhan, a student with violence deeply imbedded in his ideological but psychotic brain, enjoys Hitler-status in Mulligan's parliament. 'The shagger should be strung up,' intones a voice from the stygian gloom in the corner. 'Never mind that shagger,' growls Paddy into his half-finished pint. 'The editor will be screaming for a new edition so I must get back and help out.'

12.30: lunchtime. The lads from the docks, the suits from the nearby banks, the geansies [woollen jumpers] from the civil service, two pony tails from Trinity – remember this is 1968 – arrive with sandwiches and egos (Trinity boys, only).

2.30: 'Time to go,' bellows Tommy, not meaning a word of it. [This refers to the legal requirement to close the pub for one hour, which was known as the holy hour.] The doors are locked, but an ear is cocked for the Flynner's familiar tap on the window-pane. At long last the pony tails finish their glass of lager and head back to another afternoon of intellectual navel-gazing in the big school across the road. The lads, meanwhile, stock up for the afternoon. A pint for Jockser, *ditto* plus *The Irish Times* for Butterkrust and a pint of lager and a large Scotch for Jimmy the Scot who, a few months earlier, decided rather wisely that Dublin's social life beats the crap out of Glasgow's.

Late afternoon: serenity reigns. Paddy is back, Bobby Kennedy is elevated to Saint Bob. Butterkrust has completed the crossword. Junior has brought the paper and replenished Paddy's dwindling cash flow, and the station master [Peter Roche] is in full flight after spending a day dreaming of music halls in his Tara Street eyrie.

These are but a few memories of life in a lovely pub, frozen in time on a lovely, yet sad June 6 in 1968.

Jockser is gone to his eternal reward, to a place where there are no hikes in the price of drink. So, too, has Butterkrust and Jimmy O'Connor and Paddy Flynn and a host of others who anointed this most eminent of watering holes with their own special brand of pub cred.

The next time you sup in Mulligan's, wander into the bar, and listen not to the chatter of 1996, but to the voices of all those yesterdays. Listen hard and you'll hear them – Paddy, Jockser and company, still running the gaff.[16]

7

BAROMETER

Mulligan's new owners had seen the changes wrought by the wrecking ball on Poolbeg Street and the surrounding area. During the late 1960s and early 1970s they also began to witness an equally, if not more, powerful force, but one that was demolishing attitudes and prejudices – the women's liberation movement. Its campaigners were very different from the women who had frequented Mulligan's, such as the Royalettes, many of whom had been forced into retirement with the closure of the Theatre Royal, or members of the Emerald Girls' Pipe Band, who made collections in the pub every weekend.[1]

The driving force behind the feminist cause in Ireland was Mary Kenny, a Dubliner, who joined *The Irish Press* as woman's editor from London, where she had been working on the *Evening Standard*. The editor of *The Irish Press*, Tim Pat Coogan, who hired Kenny, described her first days at the newspaper:

Mary arrived in Burgh Quay like a comet exuding in its wake a shower of flaming particles from burning bras. On the day she arrived in the place she found that no office had been provided for her and, with a stamp of her foot and a toss of her head, informed the managing editor, the formidable William J. Redmond, that she needed an office and, until one was found for her, she too could be found in Mulligan's.[2]

Kenny surrounded herself with what Coogan described as a coterie of talented young women, such as Mairín de Búrca, Anne Harris, June Levine, Nell McCafferty and Rosita Sweetman. The *Irish Press* journalist Paddy Madden maintained that women's lib started and thrived as a result of meetings held in Mulligan's, where Kenny and her fellow campaigners discussed tactics: 'Quite what the brothers Con and Tommie Cusack made of it still remains a mystery, but there can be no doubt that in Mary Kenny's day, the pub was a hotbed of ... revolutionary politics.'[3]

By the late 1960s journalists and the remainder of the pub-going population of Dublin were becoming more and more interested in hearing the views of the Cusacks and Paddy Flynn. While the winner of the last horse race, the date of a GAA fixture or the price of a pint were typical of the queries posed by customers in all pubs, those who frequented Mulligan's realised there was a goldmine of ripostes, witticisms and keen observations in store for them should they decide to ask philosophical, or even humdrum, questions at the bar. The establishment of Mulligan's as a national barometer of opinion on sport, politics and economics can be traced to the taking over of the pub by Con, Tommie and Paddy. There was a good reason for this.

The three men had ended the six-year uncertainty over

their futures with the purchase of the pub. The disappearance of this distraction meant they could relax and allow their personalities to come to the fore. Previous owners of the pub had all displayed varying degrees of business acumen, flair and resourcefulness, and Con, Tommie and Paddy followed suit, but added extra spice to sometimes enthralled, and sometimes bewildered, customers, including angle-chasing journalists. Depending on the day, on their humour and on the attitude of the customers, each was capable of springing a surprise, becoming the sage or parading the bizarre, while several customers and barmen provided a rich chorus of patter. Whatever the response or observation, it was generally thought-provoking, funny and guaranteed to be exchanged in the verbal currency of the city for some time.

The three men shared Cavan as their native county and knew each other's work patterns well, having toiled together for more than a decade. For many years, they had shared the tasks of bottling alcohol and preparing whiskey for sale in the cellar, though these jobs were replaced in the early 1960s by more efficient, factory-driven operations.

While Con was generally associated with the bar area, Tommie devoted most of his time to looking after the front and back lounges. Paddy Flynn looked on the bar as the 'real' Mulligan's. The lounge areas of No. 9 had come into existence a little under twenty years into his tenure, and he viewed these sections as more of an intrusion than an addition. He generally peeped into the lounge areas from one of the three doors connecting them to the bar, and rarely stepped fully into them.

Though the three men were equal partners, Con and Tommie treated Flynn as the boss. He retained the title of manager and was held in high esteem by the brothers. Tommie recalled being asked by Flynn to buy trays on which pints could be placed to settle. He bought silver butcher trays, which were expensive. While Flynn was delighted with the purchase, Tommie was afraid to tell Flynn the price he had paid for them for fear of being reprimanded.[4] The trays are still in use.

Tommie referred to all male customers as 'young man', regardless of age. He held his temper well and used his natural authority to quell the noise of loud exchanges. If customers were getting out of hand, he adopted a parental or soothing tone to great effect. These same customers would, depending on the circumstance, be faced with the quiet but powerful rebuke: 'Now, now, I'm sure your parents didn't bring you up to insult people.' Tommie's pert interventions extinguished the fuse of potentially explosive rows. Customers who ignored Tommie's polite requests found themselves at the centre of unwanted attention in the midst of a silent pub, with the only escape being the door held open by Tommie, uttering the devastating goodbye: 'Come on now, you've had enough. Plenty more time to drink tomorrow, if you want. There's a good man.'

Tommie had a habit of addressing regulars by a special name, which only he might use for them. This moniker might be the part played by an actor in a television soap opera, such as 'Sergeant' for Paul Bennett after the character he portrayed in the RTÉ series *Glenroe*; a person's native county, such as 'Offaly's in again'; a physical attribute, 'Well, big man'; or related to their hobby – 'Florida Pearl' for Kris Callaghan, a racing fan who numbered the Irish-bred racehorse among her favourites. He also did not like to see women without a seat. Many men at the bar, who stood up for a moment, would find that their stool had been requisitioned by Tommie. Any objection to this would be dismissed with, 'It's for a woman.' The stool-less customers were generally at a loss as to how to argue against this without appearing ungentlemanly or unmanly.

If a customer, well known to him, began imparting some yarn about the harvest or the machinations of the Cavan county football team, Tommie would look down and listen intently, appearing shy. When the story ended, Tommie would lift his head and smile boyishly. Customers waited for his reaction. Having popped the change into the till, Tommie invariably responded with: 'Ah, that's the way it is now.'

He also had a unique way of turning down requests for loans or a free drink from customers who had no intention of honouring the debt. While it was not unusual for Mulligan's to give drink 'on tick', Tommie did not like to be made a fool of by people who continually said they would pay later but never did. On one occasion Tommie was standing on a chair, winding the clock behind the bar in the front lounge. A customer with an unrivalled reputation for borrowing and forgetting attempted to get Tommie into conversation so that he might later drop in the request for yet another loan.

'Do you have to wind the clock every day, Tommie?' the customer asked.

'Ah yeah,' Tommie replied, his attention focused entirely on the task in hand. 'No tick.' The message was clear.

Barman Paddy Kelly said that despite having lived in Dublin for so long, Tommie had never changed: 'He was the same man that left the farm. When Tommie would be asked where he was going on holidays he'd say: "Behind a ditch".'[5]

In the bar, Con displayed an equally distinct presence. Up to his retirement, he was always impeccably dressed in a white shirt, tie and white bartender's apron. Customers, who might have been unaware of the sign 'Singing Strictly Prohibited' in the back lounge, were left in no doubt about the house rule. This zero tolerance for rowdy behaviour or coarse language had been a tradition in the pub since the attack on John Mulligan by the coal-porter Thomas O'Keeffe in 1865. This attack precipitated the long-standing house rules in Mulligan's. Even singing came under, and to this day still comes under, the heading of forbidden behaviour in the pub.

One of the most popular members of staff was Christy Murtagh, who did odd jobs in the pub. He had a passionate interest in the GAA and could usually be found on Sundays collecting glasses with a transistor radio held to his ear, listening to the progress of his favourite team, Dublin, at Croke Park or some other GAA venue. He was generally in high spirits, despite having an over-curvature of the spine and enduring the physical difficulties that accompanied his disability.

A regular in Mulligan's decided one day to pour a pint of Guinness over Christy, thinking he was safe from a threatening response. Con, who is of a temperate and gentlemanly disposition, changed utterly. He subjected the customer to a tirade that witnesses described as akin to claps of thunder and bolts of lightning. They also described how the customer, who liked to think of himself as a hard man, began shaking with fear during the confrontation. Having been lifted and ejected from the premises, the customer was given the ultimate punishment that a pub can dole out – being barred for life. The 'life sentence' on him was also imposed by other bars in Dublin that had heard about the incident. The manner in which Con dealt with the attack on Christy served to reinforce the reputation of Mulligan's as a formidable leveller to bullies who felt they could do as they liked.

Con, Paddy and Tommie emerged as strong personalities in the Mulligan's microcosm. Customers were, at times, bemused by the division between bar and lounge, exemplified by Paddy's reluctance to set foot in any part of No. 9. At other times, they were confused by the quixotic replies or observations made by their hosts. Staff too found that their patience was tried, but generally with a touch of comic relief. It was the custom in Mulligan's before opening time to have the floors cleaned and to dry them by having the entrance doors of the bar and lounge areas open. One morning, barman

Noel Hawkins was instructed by Con to shut the doors. Noel did as he was told and Con went off. Soon after, Tommie arrived and told Noel to open the doors. He did as he was told again, only to be chastised by Con later, who ordered him to close the doors again. Noel addressed his employers: 'For f**k's sake boys, would ye ever make up your minds.' It was not the first time Noel had found himself in the midst of the door controversy, but it was the last.

The quiet and diligent work ethic of the three owners, and their familiarity with one another, often bred silence among them which was seen at times as a sign of division. However, whatever the soundness of observations postulated by the various wags at the counter concerning the dynamic 'on the other side', none could ignore the fact that the three owners laboured side by side for a quarter of a century, and that the Cusack brothers worked together on the premises for almost half a century.

Potential bartenders in Mulligan's underwent interviews with either two or three of the owners during which they faced searching questions. Not all lived up to expectations, either because they had an over-fondness for the products they served or because the day's takings were consistently out of kilter with the contents of the till. The capers of the most dubious barmen have become the stuff of legend among the pub's most avid customers. These stories spread rapidly through the city's drinking fraternity and helped to form an instantly recognisable Mulliganesque culture. Vignettes composed of surreal exchanges between staff and patrons were relayed by dockers, solicitors, journalists and printers to colleagues, family and drinking companions. Listeners, assured of a curveball anecdote unlike any other, expressed their joyfulness at learning of yet another prized tale giving rise to the much used phrase: 'Only in Mulligan's.'

One of the pub's most loyal customers over the years, Peter Roche, recalled taking an order from a barman as he was about to do some shopping. Roche suggested that perhaps, rather than a banana, an apple or a pear, the barman might like a melon. 'Oh no,' he replied, 'I can't peel them.'

A couple of advanced years, who had been enjoying a quiet drink, were summarily removed from the premises after the husband gave his wife a peck on the cheek. 'We'll have none of that in here,' the surprised couple were warned before being ejected.

The journalist Diarmaid Fleming recalled that he and his girlfriend were enjoying a similar quiet drink when they were ordered off the premises because they were not drinking fast enough. A researcher for BBC Lancashire told of how his boss had been barred from the premises in the 1970s for a fight he claimed he did not start. When his boss returned to Mulligan's some fifteen years later he was refused entry on the grounds that he had already been told that he was barred.

Two tourists from the United States enquired if it would be possible to get a sandwich and were asked what type would they like. They plumped for salad, ordered their drinks and sat down to wait for their refreshments. After much time had elapsed, one of them approached the bar and asked if the sandwiches were ready. 'We don't do food here,' the barman snapped.

The intermittent craziness of Mulligan's delighted Con Cusack's wife, Brigid, who moved into the upstairs of No. 8 after their marriage in 1969. Apart from the real-life pantomime played out every now and then below stairs, Brigid also enjoyed the village atmosphere that was still evident in the area at that time.[6] Beside Mulligan's was the saddler, Sam Greer, who had operated out of Poolbeg Street since the early twentieth century. Vestiges of earlier times manifested themselves in the presence of a number of cobblers and passing street traders such as an oyster seller. William 'Spud' Murphy recalled that in the evenings, a trumpeter would make a pit stop outside Mulligan's and play 'Oh My Papa' in the hope of receiving change from departing or arriving customers.

Despite the closure of the Theatre Royal earlier in the decade, the Mulligan's name continued to make further inroads – both great and humorous – into the Arts. In 1969 James Plunkett's sprawling novel *Strumpet City* was published. It was based around the 1913 Lock-out, an event in which the pub had played a peripheral part, and Plunkett set one of his scenes in Mulligan's.

Meanwhile, filming on the Dingle Peninsula in County Kerry of David Lean's epic, *Ryan's Daughter*, was delayed by storms and by Lean's insistence on waiting for the right kind of weather to film some sequences. During one long spell without a shoot, Arthur 'Archie' O'Sullivan, who played the part of Joe McCardle, decided he had earned a break. He hired a car and ordered the driver to take him to Mulligan's. The driver told O'Sullivan that a pub of that name did not exist in the area. O'Sullivan then informed the driver that he wanted to go to Mulligan's in Dublin. 'You're f**king coddin,' the driver replied. He drove the actor 350 kilometres (217 miles) to Dublin, where O'Sullivan had three pints of Guinness in Mulligan's before being driven back to the location in County Kerry.[7]

Mulligan's name was spreading even further afield. Julia Watson, an executive with Fontana Books, visited Dublin in 1970 to promote some of the publisher's titles at a reception in the Gresham Hotel in O'Connell Street. During the function, Ms Watson asked Noel Conway, a journalist with *The Irish Press*, to take her to Mulligan's 'just to have a close look at what a real Irish pint looks like'. As Conway recalled, soon after arriving in Mulligan's, a pint of Guinness was placed in front of her:

> Julia looked, then sipped and ended by downing the lot. The barman gave her a look of admiration.
>
> Giving the counter a wipe of his cloth he told her: 'You are an English colleen [*sic*] now. You've got Irish blood in you.'
>
> She turned to me: 'You know, if we stay here much longer I'll feel like writing a book myself.' Mulligan's has that sort of effect on one. May it never change.[8]

In 1970 the Corn Exchange building, which had provided much of Mulligan's turnover since 1815, was sold to a consortium, which developed the premises into apartment blocks and offices. Although the Corn Exchange had ceased to be a neighbourhood boon to Mulligan's for decades, its sale marked the disappearance of yet another important building that had, in previous times, fed the pub's reserves.[9]

While the end of the Corn Exchange marked another depletion in the character of the vicinity, inside Mulligan's tradition prevailed, particularly regarding the unexpected. Patrick O'Brien, a potter, recalled leaving his ham behind by mistake in the pub two days before Christmas. He called back on Christmas Eve, when Tommie Cusack chastised him for being so careless. The ham was handed back ready for eating. Tommie's wife, Evelyn, had steeped the ham at home the night before.[10]

Mulligan's attracted an eclectic mix of customers in the 1970s. A journalist in the *Catholic Herald*, writing in 1990, described the clientèle:

> When I lived and worked in Dublin 20 years ago or so, [Mulligan's] was the almost daily meeting place of the boss of the Dublin police, a prominent race-horse owner, the fire chief, several rich businessmen, the 'corner boys' whose street cries as paper vendors were – and still are – a feature of Dublin life, and many other excellent characters, including a certain William Shakespeare, head photographer at the *Irish Press*.[11]

The *Irish Press* journalist Michael O'Toole claimed that Shakespeare's father, Joe, one of the newspaper's early photographers, named his son William to ensure that no one would ever give him a job as a reporter.[12]

Aodhan Madden, another journalist with *The Irish Press*, described the newspaper people who frequented the pub as cynics. Some of these customers were sub-editors working on *The Irish Press*. Each had his eccentricities. One brought into the office home-made 'fry' sandwiches consisting of two ugly lumps of bread clamped over a fried egg, black pudding and a tomato which 'he fed upon with the fury of a barracuda'. Another binned a breaking news story about the Six-Day War because he had to catch the four o'clock bus home to Bray, where he kept a guesthouse.[13]

The editor of *The Irish Press*, Tim Pat Coogan, remembered an incident when the newspaper's circulation manager, Paddy Cregan, asked him for a meeting to discuss a difficulty he was having. They decided to meet in Mulligan's. On Cregan's arrival, he noticed many members of his staff drinking in the bar. There was a general scatter as someone shouted, 'Cregan's in.' One of the workers decided that he was not going to be intimidated by the presence of his boss, announcing that he did not care who was in the bar. He turned around and, as he faced Cregan's blazing blue eyes, he promptly fell off his stool.[14]

The odd mix of people in Mulligan's fuelled its reputation as a pub of character and its name kept seeping into the unlikeliest of places. In December 1972 the Social and Personal column in *The Irish Times* announced that the President had received His Excellency, the Most Rev. Gaetano Alibrandi,

Apostolic Nuncio. Another entry told readers of the engagement of Mr P. A. A. Dudgeon to Miss P. R. Batchen. Among this august company was another notice:

> B. D. Usher, Esq., has returned to town. Festivities as usual in Mulligan's, Poolbeg Street.[15]

8

A Tribute to Con

Con Houlihan began working for the *Evening Press* in 1974. The date of the start of his association with Mulligan's is not known. With ink from one and liquor from the other he spread the fame of both. In his back-page column he generally divided the introductory paragraph and the remainder with the beckoning: 'Now read on.' Readers who obeyed were led by his big hand on a meandering journey.

During his two decades with the *Evening Press* and another decade writing for the *Sunday World* and *Evening Herald*, Houlihan became as well known for his connection with Mulligan's as he did for his journalism. Other pubs in Dublin and elsewhere in Ireland can legitimately claim Houlihan as a regular. However, none can claim to have had a more well-known or special relationship than that which he had with Mulligan's. The pub was mentioned more often in his writings than any other. This connection was reinforced by his presence in Mulligan's on big and small sporting occasions. People saw his giant frame when they arrived on the premises. He became part of the furniture of the pub. During his lifetime, this connection was firmly established in the public mind. Since his death, this link has not diminished. The union was underlined in a documentary about him, *Waiting for Houlihan*, in 2012 and in a series of special supplements published by the *Irish Independent* in February and March 2013. The relationship was akin to that of Joyce and Dublin. Houlihan and Mulligan's were blessed by knowing and raising a toast to each other. The story of Mulligan's would be incomplete without a tribute to its most cherished patron.

Houlihan was born outside Castle Island (which he maintained should be two words) in County Kerry on 6 December 1925. His father, Michael, left school at twelve years of age and his mother, Helen, when she was thirteen. They met while working for the same farmer. On the day of their wedding they had to hand-milk thirty cows before they went to the church. Houlihan said his father was 'very fond of the drink', a characteristic he inherited.[1] His mother bestowed on him a love of literature. She felt life had passed her by and was, as a result, academically ambitious for her children. Houlihan, a middle child, had one brother, Diarmuid, and one sister, Marie. The family had five acres of land and sixteen of bog.

Con started school at the age of seven and showed early promise as a scholar. When he was eleven years old he began to board at Castlemartyr College, near Youghal in County Cork, from where he was later expelled for publishing what he described as 'seditious' articles in the school magazine.[2] He then attended the Christian Brothers School in Tralee before enrolling in a school in Castle Island, where he sat his Leaving Certificate examination at the age of fifteen.

Having earned a little money as a casual labourer in the local bogs, he went to London in 1943, where he worked in the East End clearing the rubble of houses and other buildings that had been bombed during the Second World War. Two years later, he returned home and enrolled for a general Arts degree at University College, Cork. While at university, he advanced his knowledge of English, history, Latin and mathematics. He graduated four years later with a first class honours degree. He earned money during this time by making black puddings for Charlie Lenihan, a butcher in Castle Island. Having completed an MA in English, he went to England again, teaching in a prep school in Hastings for two years before returning home.

Charlie Lenihan, the butcher for whom he had worked, founded a newspaper, the *Taxpayers' News*, and installed Houlihan as editor. Houlihan also worked in various local primary schools and supplemented his income by correcting Leaving Certificate honours English and Latin papers and by giving private tuition. One of his students, Mike Kenny, recalled that Houlihan taught him differential calculus: 'Now I was never mathematically inclined at all but whatever gift he had we were able to do it.'[3]

Houlihan was sought out by Tony Meade, assistant editor of *The Kerryman*, to write for the newspaper. Meade recalled that Houlihan wrote his articles on butcher paper which, he presumed, had originated in Charlie Lenihan's shop. Houlihan also scripted over thirty radio and television documentaries on the GAA, on traditional music and, more frequently, on his beloved Kerry. In 1974 he worked with the film director, Pat O'Connor, to make a short documentary, *The Wheels of the World – Life in North Kerry*. That year also saw Houlihan, who was at that time living in Dublin, take up an invitation from the editor of the *Evening Press*, Seán Ward, and his colleague, Liam Flynn, to write as a freelancer for the newspaper. He began by contributing one column a week on sport, which increased to three columns shortly afterwards. After two years, he began writing another, fortnightly, column called 'Tributaries' for the newspaper, which was based on his interests in literature and history.

No profile of Con Houlihan appeared without a mention of his appearance or mannerisms, both of which, intentionally or unintentionally, drew notice. He was very tall and broad-shouldered. His wild hair gave the impression that it had never undergone the discipline of a comb. His face was that of a countryman who had been ravaged by bog winds and warmed before a turf fire. He spoke in a high-pitched voice and in a strong Kerry brogue that was difficult for many people to decipher. Generally, he held up his left or right hand to his face when he spoke, sometimes touching his nose with an index finger or using his hand as a shield against eavesdroppers to deliver his message uniquely to his talking companion. His clothing normally included tracksuit bottoms, a jumper, an anorak and runners/sneakers, all of which had seen better days.

His method of writing was to pen a paragraph on a single sheet of paper and then move on to the next sheet.

He stopped regularly and put his two big outstretched hands over his face to help him concentrate. Colleagues in the *Irish Press* building rarely arrived before he did. Houlihan attended a match, play or other event and then went drinking. After a few hours' sleep he rose at around half past four in the morning and began writing his column. He worked fifty-two weeks of the year throughout his twenty-one-year association with the *Evening Press*, except for the two years he spent in Kerry looking after his dying mother.

Tony Meade of *The Kerryman* described Houlihan's writing style as deceptively simple: 'He was a stylist. I often felt that what he was capable of doing with words and with syntax was somewhat wasted in writing columns in newspapers – that he was capable of something much better'.[4]

The *Sunday Independent* columnist Declan Lynch, who conducted a memorable interview with Houlihan for *Hot Press* in 1984, wrote in 2012 about his attraction to Houlihan's back-page column in the *Evening Press*:

> Each paragraph was written in longhand on a separate page, his choice of longhand partly dictated by the fact that his fingers were so big they would get stuck in the keys of a typewriter. So he would dash off these dozens of pages, often under the most terrifying deadline pressure, and yet always with that attention to detail which you will find in Con's own declaration that 'a man who can put an apostrophe in the wrong place is capable of anything'.[5]

Houlihan compared the exercise of writing to a form of drug: 'Writing is my therapy. If tomorrow morning I am feeling guilty, depressed or just plain terrible, I will sit down and maybe I will think of a good sentence and it starts from there. It's my heroin, my Valium.'[6]

One of Houlihan's most memorable columns was his report on the 1978 All-Ireland football final between Dublin and Kerry. Journalist Eoghan Corry encouraged readers to close their eyes and put Houlihan's images into their head: 'It is magnificent. I think it is one of the great images of that entire era in Irish sports journalism':[7]

> The drizzling rain seemed irrelevant as Dublin moved the ball with the confidence of a grandmaster playing chess against a novice. After 25 minutes, Dublin led by 6 points to 1. It did not flatter them but perhaps it's true that whom the Gods wish to destroy they first make mad. The ease with which Dublin were scaling the mountain seduced them into over-confidence.

A free was awarded to Kerry, which drew objections from the Dublin players:

> Paddy [Cullen] put on a show of righteous indignation that would get him a card from Equity [the actors' union]. As this was going on, Mike Sheehy was coming up to take the kick and suddenly Paddy dashed back towards his goal like a woman who smells a cake burning.

The ball won the race and it curled inside the near post as Paddy crashed into the outside of the net and lay against it like a fireman who had returned to find his station ablaze.[8]

Houlihan's column regularly concluded with a brief comment, *Fógra* (notice), *Fógra eile* (another notice) or *Agus Fógra eile* (and another notice), in which he congratulated young athletes on their achievements, commiserated with bereaved families or encouraged other writers.

His insight for sport was equalled by his knowledge of politics, history and literature. He was a strong critic of the IRA and of Charles Haughey from an early stage in his writing career.[9] When he scoffed at the failings of politicians or the political system, he did so with inventiveness, humour and a great deal of style.

Constantine P. Cavafy, Sherwood Anderson, Anton Chekhov and Thomas Hardy were among his favourite writers. He had a particular affection and admiration for the poetry of Patrick Kavanagh and wrote glowingly about him. However, when the two met in the Bailey pub in Dublin, Kavanagh felt that Houlihan had been condescending and described him as 'the biggest pygmy in Ireland'.[10]

Houlihan's own views on well-known and respected people in Irish society sometimes went against the grain. He described Dr Noël Browne as 'one of the great egoists of our time'; the poet, Seamus Heaney, as 'a great self-propagandist'; and he accused the author, broadcaster and sports analyst, Éamon Dunphy, of thinking that 'if you're nasty you'll be great'.[11] He also described Brian Friel's *Translations* as 'a sentimental play bordering on "melodrama"'.

His creative juices and sensitivity caused him unease, which he described frankly in an interview with *In Dublin* magazine in 1989:

> In his few hours of slumber he admits to having several 'mad recurring dreams'. Their contents are evidence of a man terribly unsure of himself and of his great talents. One is of himself out fishing and every fish he catches is rotten and hideously deformed. 'This is telling me that what I'm writing is rotten too, that it's rubbish.' Another has him naked and thoroughly abashed in a public place.[12]

His views were also unconventional. He regarded religion as 'the curse of the world, I hate it and deplore it even though some of my best friends are nuns and priests'. He was antagonistic towards the institution of marriage:

> I can love 40 girls at one time. At present I have a girlfriend. This belief that you meet a girl, have intercourse and get married – it's a total lie. I could be fond of 40, 50 girls and my girlfriend could be too.[13]

To him, freedom was 'going out of an evening and being able to speak your mind without getting a belt'. He defined democracy in the context of his experience of a café he used to frequent near the Strand Palace hotel in London:

Peter's café has a little counter and six scrubbed wooden tables. It is the kind of place where you can be asked for the loan of your spoon – that, to me, is the essence of democracy.[14]

Houlihan's witticisms were numerous. His friend Ray Hennessy recalled a comment Houlihan made when unable to locate a book of poetry by Gerald Manley Hopkins after a cleaning woman had been at the house: 'You know, if that woman worked in Trinity College she'd throw out the Book of Kells'.[15]

The former Minister for the Arts, and former Kerry footballer, Jimmy Deenihan remembers that before the 1975 All-Ireland football final, he (Deenihan) was quoted in the *Irish Independent* as saying, 'Kerry will win because we are more natural footballers than Dublin.' Con noted Deenihan's remarks and waited until after the 1976 All-Ireland – which Dublin won – to comment. In his column, he asked if Deenihan meant that Dublin were unnatural footballers and reminded him that 'you should never cast aspersions on the alligator's mother before crossing the river'.[16]

After a budding screenwriter with an inflated sense of his own importance had not been seen for some time, locals in Mulligan's presumed he had left for Hollywood. Houlihan, who had spotted him in Dublin, remarked: 'Forgotten but not gone.'

The journalist Paul Melia observed that Houlihan's theatre criticism, while never malicious, could deliver a put-down when required: 'On hearing that a theatre company complained about him snoring during a play, he replied that it was a shame the audience was required to stay awake for it.'[17]

While Houlihan was covering the European soccer championships, held during a very hot summer in West Germany in 1988, there was much discussion in Mulligan's about how he would deal with the oppressive weather. When he returned, barman Paddy Kelly overheard one of a party of Dublin soccer fans questioning Houlihan about this:

> *Dublin soccer fan*: Jaysus Con, how in the name of Jaysus did you stick that f**king anorak on you out there?
>
> *Con*: I'll tell you one thing now boy. Did your father never tell you what keeps out the cold also keeps out the heat?[18]

Having completed or put the final touches to his back-page column at the *Irish Press* building, Houlihan was ready for his odyssey around the city, as the columnist John Boland recalled:

> By 9 a.m., he was gone to embrace the day and all its myriad possibilities – and the night, too, where he could be found absorbed in animated conversation in the Silver Swan or the Scotch House on Burgh Quay or in Mulligan's of Poolbeg Street or in a variety of other hostelries unknown to all but the true connoisseur of chat and craic.[19]

Gary Cusack, the present co-owner of Mulligan's, said that Houlihan normally came into the pub at around midday and had a nap in the corner. Gary recalled that: 'If anybody came in looking for him, Da [Tommie Cusack] would say he was sleeping and not available.'[20] While Houlihan was on first-name terms with many publicans, he had a particular fondness for Con and Tommie Cusack, both of whom he noted, 'ran a good ship'.[21] He liked the banter of GAA rivalry and often maintained to the Cavan-born brothers that he was sure they had a case of champagne in the cellar in case their team won the All-Ireland, before adding that he was also sure it was safe from consumption for a little while more. He did not use a bank and left all his money in the Mulligan's safe in the cellar. His float was kept in a glass tankard in the front lounge. Houlihan described the arrangement as his 'Cavan bank'.

Houlihan wrote many articles on Mulligan's, several of which concerned barmen, owners or customers who had died. However, he also regularly made brief mention of the pub in his columns. Houlihan's lengthiest article on the pub was devoted to other eccentricities and eccentrics who drank there:

> There are two bars in Mulligan's, facing each other: the printers drank in the left-hand bar; the journalists drank in the right-hand side. I could never puzzle out which was looking down on the other, all I knew was that they were both looking across at each other. I had colleagues who wouldn't dream of being seen on the other side; I had colleagues who wouldn't dream of being seen in Mulligan's at all.[22]

Many of Houlihan's characteristics and habits had peculiarities attached to them. When he played rugby in his early life, he did so in bare feet. For a man who was well able to communicate through his writing, he lacked clarity in conversation. When attending sports events he avoided the press box, always standing amongst the spectators. Though he was well known as a drinker, he paced himself and embarked on journeys around Dublin and other cities more in search of conversation than alcohol. In fact, his drinking too had its unique side. His favourite tipple was brandy and milk: 'The brandy takes the *shting* out of the milk.'[23] Having been brought up in a family that had little, he did not succumb to thriftiness in later life and was generous with money, to an astounding degree, with taxi-drivers, bartenders and friends.

Houlihan and Mulligan's found themselves with too much in common not to have become intertwined. One was rarely mentioned without the other. The man and the institution became surreal reflected images of one another. Despite the strength of character of both, there was never a falling out. The strange orbits of the earthly worlds of Houlihan and Mulligan's intersected regularly; the level of fame these crossings achieved was, as Houlihan himself might have put it, 'astronomical'.

During Houlihan's association with the *Evening Press*, which began in 1974, he was linked intrinsically with Mulligan's. A photograph of him and his writings adorn the walls of the pub. As a nomadic landmark, Houlihan spread his love for the grand old pub of Poolbeg Street in his writing and in his conversation.

9

DOUBLE CENTURY

The Troubles, which began in the late 1960s, found expression in Poolbeg Street in the early 1970s.[1] The *Irish Press* building was the subject of several bomb alerts.[2] When this happened its occupants were forced to vacate the offices, and some sought refuge in Mulligan's.

In this tense atmosphere, one of the pub's best-known regulars, Mick Byrne, known as Butterkrust, became the unwilling centre of attention during a security alert in Mulligan's. Byrne, who worked as a janitor at the offices of the Workers' Union of Ireland some distance away in Parnell Square, had parked his bicycle outside the pub. A brown parcel of sticks in the carrier caught the attention of a passer-by, who notified the gardaí. Staff and customers were cleared from the pub as officers and members of the army bomb disposal team took up positions on Poolbeg Street. Byrne took his time leaving and was the last to emerge from the pub. Wiping the froth from his mouth, he mounted his bicycle and cycled off, whistling, as the assembled security forces looked at each other in surprise.[3] Mulligan's propensity for attaching itself uncannily to moments in Irish history was showing no signs of abating.

Peter Roche, the then stationmaster at Tara Street, established his reputation as one of Mulligan's stalwarts when he initiated the pub's Christmas draw in 1974. The draw, which continues to this day, has become a staple of life in Mulligan's in December, drawing interest from regulars, GAA fans, bar staff in pubs throughout Dublin and tourists. By the time Roche established the draw, he already had a long association with Mulligan's, having been a regular visitor to the Theatre Royal and an avid collector of autographs and pictures of the stars who performed there and at other theatres. While many writers credited or referred to Con Houlihan as Mulligan's public relations officer, Houlihan himself always insisted that Peter Roche held the honour uniquely. Roche, known by his initials PR and as 'Dr Roche', became a close and long-term friend of Houlihan, whom he credited with having reintroduced him to the All-Ireland football finals in the 1970s.

The fierce clashes between Kerry and, generally, Dublin at the time drew people to watch Gaelic football who had never shown any interest in it before. The encounters also attracted readers to Houlihan's column. His obvious love and support for Kerry served to make him more readable, even to Dublin supporters, who showed an immediate liking for his style.

The Kerry–Dublin encounters on the pitch always had a sequel in Mulligan's. The relationship between the two sets of supporters was generally good-humoured. The actor, Jer O'Leary, recalled that his brother, Denis A. O'Leary, a diehard Dublin fan, got into a lively argument about one

Seán O'Donohoe, who, at ninety years of age, is Mulligan's oldest surviving former bartender. *Courtesy of Jack O'Donohoe*

Former Mulligan's bartender Paddy (P. J.) Kelly, who served some of the pub's most famous customers.

Former Mulligan's bartender Tommy McDonald holding one of his most prized possessions, a ticket for the 1947 Football All-Ireland final which his native County Cavan won. *Courtesy of Eileen McDonald*

The journalist Jack Grealish, who accompanied John F. Kennedy to Mulligan's in 1947. *Courtesy of Anthony Grealish*

The author and journalist Con Houlihan beside Mulligan's famous grandfather clock. *Photo by Colman Doyle, by kind permission of the National Library of Ireland*

The present co-owners of Mulligan's, brothers Ger and Gary Cusack.
Courtesy of Collins Photos, Dublin

Former owners of Mulligan's, Tommie Cusack, Paddy Flynn and Tommie's brother, Con. *Photo by Colman Doyle, by kind permission of the National Library of Ireland*

Mulligan's regulars William 'Spud' Murphy, Robert Sweeney, Peter Roche and Richard Whyte. *Courtesy of Collins Photos, Dublin*

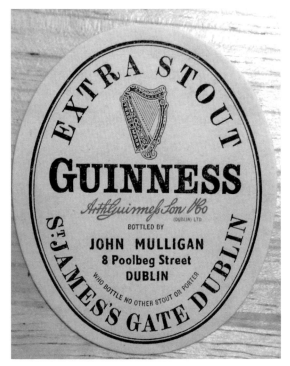

One of the labels with the Mulligan's name and address that were pasted onto Guinness bottles by pub staff up to the 1960s.

Signature of Nicholas Schults, who built the premises housing Mulligan's today, from a deed dated 1750. *Courtesy of the Registry of Deeds, Dublin*

Token struck by one of Mulligan's original owners, Talbot Fyan, in 1794, which was used as a supplement to legitimate coinage.

Mulligan's bartenders Mick McGovern, Billy Phelan and Christy Hynes picketing the premises during a strike for better pay and conditions in 1994. *Courtesy of The Irish Press*

Signwriter Richard Levins putting the finishing touches to Mulligan's façade in August 2014.

Billy Brooks Carr, right, leading the All-Bones Marching Band at the St Patrick's Day Parade in Houston, Texas, in 1985. Some of Billy's ashes are encased in Mulligan's grandfather clock. *Photo taken by Tom Foley, courtesy of the Carr family*

Christy Hynes, one of four Mulligan's barmen who have reported para-normal activity on the premises.

Mulligan's barman Noel Hawkins.

Robert Sweeney raising a glass in front of the plaque to the author and journalist Con Houlihan. *Courtesy of Collins Photos, Dublin*

Christy Murphy, a Mulligan's regular, whose photograph in Mulligan's has the legend 'Computers how are ye'.
Photo by Colman Doyle, by kind permission of the National Library of Ireland

Mulligan's getting a make-over in the summer of 2014.
Courtesy of Collins Photos, Dublin

All-Ireland final with an equally stalwart Kerry supporter, Mairéad O'Connor from Killorglin. Shortly afterwards they fell in love and married.

It was in this busy pub that Ger Cusack began working when he was fourteen years old, under the stewardship of his father, Tommie, and uncle, Con. Customers attempted to confuse the teenager by asking if the pub sold brandy on draught. Whatever naivety was present when he arrived, it soon evaporated. For a lounge-boy, as for a barman, Mulligan's was a 'sink or swim' pub.

The contrast between Mulligan's and its vicinity was stark. In a profile of the area, *The Irish Times* described Mulligan's as the only trace of humanity left in Poolbeg Street.[4] The soulless 1960s architecture had by then suffocated any other charm the street had once had.

Inside Mulligan's, Ger Cusack was presented with another very different picture of life. The pub was used as a location for a film based on James Joyce's book *A Portrait of the Artist as a Young Man*, directed by Joseph Strick. *The Irish Press* reported that no structural changes to the pub were necessary for filming, but the shelves were cleared and replaced with the 1900s-type large Guinness bottles and a set of pint-pulling pumps was put in place. The scene shot in Mulligan's was meant to be in Cork, but Strick had no difficulty with this anomaly: 'I decided on Mulligan's for the scene, not only because of the excellent interior which suits the period, but also because there seems to be a curious Cork atmosphere in the place.'[5]

As a young boy, Ger had been used to exploring, with his siblings, the pub's nooks and crannies and its creepy cellars. He noticed the difference between the pub during its hectic opening hours and when it was closed. In the quiet times, the bar and lounge areas in semi-darkness took on an eerie and even sinister quality when its unique sounds – some identifiable, others inexplicable – manifested themselves.

Ger also identified some of the layers of attraction that drew customers. It had obvious appeal to GAA supporters – most notably when Dublin footballers were playing in Croke Park – that invariably resulted in Poolbeg Street turning into a sea of blue as fans crowded into it. However, Ger also became aware of the regular return visits by supporters of the then rugby Five Nations Championship. He recalled the greetings exchanged between his father and English, French, Scottish and Welsh rugby fans as they arrived for their biennial visits. While support for the Republic of Ireland national soccer team had not reached the level it attained in the late 1980s and 1990s, many customers, including Butterkrust, were among some of its all-weather supporters who frequented Mulligan's in the 1970s.

National newspapers continued their preoccupation with chivvying out mentions of Mulligan's in unlikely places. The diarist, Seamus Kelly, writing under his pseudonym 'Quidnunc' in *The Irish Times*, gave a list of toasts being offered by a group on a pre-Christmas pub crawl of thirty-nine drinking establishments in Belfast. They included Her Majesty the Queen, His Holiness the Pope, Humphrey

Bogart, Mulligan's of Poolbeg Street, and big-bosomed ladies.[6]

Magill magazine provided an insight into the make-up of the clientèle during several rhetorical flourishes in a review of pubs in 1978:

> Some people would like to put a preservation order on this pub and its atmosphere. Devoid of plastic trimmings, fulfilling its function as a place to meet and drink in much the way that old Wild West saloons must have done, it's a natural for those who are into basic living, maaaan. Unfortunately, it attracts its share of those who make a pretention of unpretentiousness and, on a crowded night, you're liable to wind up next to a Trinity student brandishing his cut price copy of *The Irish Times*, dipping his scarf into your drink and emoting about *Annie Hall* in a voice that sounds like all his teeth are loose. However, the simplicity of the place is attractive and, as long as you've brought your own good company, does it really matter that those three gesticulators in the corner are pseuds or geniuses?[7]

Noel Hawkins, who joined Mulligan's in 1979, found a broader range of customers. His father and grandfather, who had worked on the docks, had been regulars in the pub. Tommie Cusack made the connection between father and son while he and Con Cusack interviewed Noel. He was hired. Having worked in the bar trade for the previous two years, he was not exactly a greenhorn, but his first impression of Mulligan's was the courtesy of the customers: 'They said "please" and "thank you". I had not been used to that in the bar I came from.'

Noel also noticed the division that existed among customers: 'If you drank in the lounge, you drank in the lounge. If you drank in the bar, you drank in the bar.' His colleague Christy Hynes said that this division is almost gone today, but shades of it remain even with the staff: 'I work in the bar. I'm like a tourist in the lounge. I don't know where anything is.'[8]

One of Noel's tasks was to stop traffic in Poolbeg Street as Paddy Flynn drove his car out of the gateway from the courtyard of No. 10. The extreme care taken by Paddy contrasted with the way in which Con Cusack entered and left the courtyard in his Mercedes, oblivious to scrapes that generally ensued from the manoeuvre.[9]

Noel also endured the flights of mischief taken by Con Cusack who, on one occasion, told him to refuse to serve a customer – whose arm was broken and in a cast – knowing full well the reaction it would elicit:

> I told [the customer] he couldn't have any more drink and he said: 'How dare you! I have never been so insulted in all my life. I shall never drink here again', and then he banged his broken arm on the counter and broke it again.[10]

However, he found that some customers needed no encouragement to be stirred into a frenzy; they were quite capable of managing this all on their own:

> There were two married couples who drank together. One of the wives sneezed, whereupon her husband put his hand in

his pocket to produce a handkerchief and it was a pair of red knickers and she said 'That's not mine', and chased him round the bar for a while, hitting him with her handbag. That was very funny.[11]

The colourful mix of customers included John Flood, a musician who was granted permission to play the clarinet in Mulligan's on Sundays before Christmas. Another well-known visitor was Arthur Fields, known as 'The Man on the Bridge', who, for decades, trod O'Connell Street taking pictures of passers-by which they could later purchase for a small fee. Noel also recalls that Sinéad O'Connor drank in Mulligan's early in her career. So too did members of U2 when they were trying to make a name for themselves.

One prominent group of customers, who frequented Mulligan's during the first years of Noel's tenure, situated themselves at the back of the bar area. The group comprised Fred Ludlow, John O'Connor, Tony Power, George Pujolas and his brother Tommy, and Louis Robinson, who had kept an old train ticket to Belfast, where he had gone, he claimed, to take part in a manoeuvre linked to the 1916 Rising. These six customers named the area where they drank as Nuts' Corner, a designation that area of the bar has retained.[12]

Noel soon became known for his quick wit and his capacity to deliver a succession of jokes, amusing stories and anecdotes. The serving areas behind the bar and lounge counters became a stage where he performed at the drop of a beer mat to local and international customers. Visitors from the United States, in particular, regarded him as the epitome of an Irish bartender. On return journeys to Ireland, Mulligan's was always high on their list of destinations to visit.

Billy Brooks Carr became one of thousands of tourists from the United States attracted by the magnetism of Mulligan's. He first arrived with his younger brother, Mike, in October 1980. They made other pilgrimages to the pub with Billy's twin brother, David, in later years. Billy was a proud Irish-American who enjoyed the spectacle of St Patrick's Day parades in Houston, many of which he marched in. He was a self-taught musician who played the bones and founded the All-Bones Marching Band. The three brothers were famous locally for having scored a hole-in-one on separate occasions on the fourteenth hole at the Clear Creek golf course, Fellows Road, Houston. They ran a bar, Mama Hattie's (called after their grandmother) in Humble, Texas. When a building next door became available, they bought it and crafted the new bar in the likeness of Mulligan's. One of the reasons for this was that Billy regarded the Guinness he had been served in the Dublin Mulligan's to be the best he had ever consumed.[13]

Mulligan's reputation for serving the best pint of Guinness was long established. Repeated efforts by representatives of Guinness's competitors, including Beamish, to get the pub to sell its product were met with a blank refusal by Tommie Cusack, who was insistent that Mulligan's was a Guinness pub.[14] Beamish was most persistent about placing its product in Mulligan's, going so far as to hire a bus to take the pub's customers to another area of the city, where they were offered free pints of Beamish. This campaign stopped after a few weeks, however, when the company representatives found that after having their fill of Beamish, the customers made their way back to Mulligan's where they returned to drinking Guinness.

The pub's reputation for its quality of Guinness and the variety of custom it attracted were enhanced by continued publicity in the national and international media. In its hundredth issue, *In Dublin* magazine published a list of '100 reasons to be cheerful' one of which was the 'niceties of the pint and small one in Mulligan's'.[15]

In 1982 the organisers of Bloomsday on 16 June – the date around which events in James Joyce's novel *Ulysses* revolve – installed in Mulligan's an actor to play Joyce and to answer questions from journalists.[16] The year marked the centenary of Joyce's birth and the bicentenary of the premises as a pub, a milestone that the Cusacks, in typical quirky Mulligan's fashion, decided to ignore. *The New York Times* described Mulligan's as a pub that had 'held on to its aura, especially in the back parlour where the student Joyce often sat'.[17]

Writers, artists, politicians and athletes regularly dropped in to Mulligan's to meet Con Houlihan. In 1983 he was interviewed by a young journalist, Colum McCann, who was on a work experience programme with the *Connaught Telegraph*, to discover his views on the forthcoming Connacht football final between Galway and Mayo.[18] McCann, who has since become a best-selling novelist, recalled:

Con's big hands on the bar, the slow pull of the pint, the rough edge of the counter, the hard music of *Irish Press* printers sending pints up along the bar. And Con, putting his arm around me, telling me about the writing life: 'You create life out of life, say things all over again.'[19]

Other less welcome visitors to Mulligan's were a reflection of the upsurge in crime and in the number of criminal gangs engulfing Dublin in the 1980s. Mulligan's experienced the effects of both small- and large-scale offenders. Neither found any luck on the premises.

One morning, Tommie Cusack arrived at the pub and began putting the finishing touches to cleaning the premises before opening. In the toilet off the bar area, he noticed cigarette butts on the floor of one of the cubicles. There was no one in either cubicle. He had swept the area before locking up the night before and knew they had not been there at that time. Apparently, an intruder had climbed into the attic through a trapdoor in the ceiling before closing time the previous evening. His intentions were unclear. However, he left with as much as he had come in with, though he did leave a legacy in Mulligan's – from that time there has been a padlock on the trapdoor in the toilet ceiling.[20]

Another crime, which had its conclusion in Mulligan's, involved Mickey Boyle and his accomplice, Eugene Prunty, who spent much of the summer of 1983 logging the movements of a wealthy solicitor, William Somerville, as he came and went from his house in Dargle Hill near Enniskerry in County Wicklow, as recounted by Paul Williams in his book, *Badfellas*.[21] Boyle and Prunty eventually kidnapped Mr Somerville and demanded a ransom of £50,000 from his family for his release. The Somerville family alerted the gardaí, who mounted a search for the kidnappers. Prunty was arrested in Bray, County Wicklow. The gardaí later caught up with Boyle, who was wearing a wig and sunglasses:

> The arrest was made in Mulligan's pub in Poolbeg Street. The gardaí appeared to be following the man and, when he went into the pub, some stood guard at the two entrance doors while others went inside. The man had just gone to the public telephone and was using it when he was surrounded by about half a dozen detectives.
>
> One pulled a brown wig off the man's partially bald head and said he was arresting him under section 30 of the Offences Against the State Act.[22]

In an interview Paddy Flynn gave in 1983, he lamented the demise of the Theatre Royal and the consequent disappearance of the type of customers it had brought to Mulligan's. By this time he had also reduced his workload to just doing the books:

> The old chest was at me and, when I went to the doctor, he said I had to give up the smokes. When I told him I never smoked in my life he was astonished. It seems that the smoke that everyone else smoked in all the years I was there did the

trick. In a way, I'm just as glad I'm at the books. When I serve the odd pint it breaks my heart not to give a man back change out of a pound.[23]

10

MULLIGAN'S IN PRINT

Customers were not shy in making known their feelings on changes proposed or made by the owners of Mulligan's. The laying of a carpet in the front and back lounges in 1988 caused consternation. Con Cusack reckoned that the floor furnishing was the biggest change made in the pub in a half century.[1] The owners decided to impose a one penny increase on the price of the pint to help pay for the carpet, which had cost £7,000 in Clerys department store. Barmen had to endure the wrath of patrons, who argued that they had no need of a carpet but much need of the money it was now costing to drink in Mulligan's.[2] Conservationists also raised objections, because they felt it was an unacceptable adjustment to the interior of the 200-year-old building.

Such was the storm of protest directed at the Cusacks and Flynn, they believed that Mulligan's 'would be kicked out of all the guide books'.[3] The *Irish Press* columnist Barbara McKeown celebrated the new furnishing by kicking off her shoes and dancing up and down the bar in the front lounge.[4] Con Houlihan believed the carpet had been laid 'so that people couldn't hear coins falling', adding a dart at the reputation for thriftiness of the owners' native county: 'By now you have guessed, it is a Cavan establishment.'[5]

In an interview with *The Irish Times*, Con Cusack reflected on the changes he had seen during his three decades in Mulligan's. He recalled that when he started in 1950, £1 would buy thirty pints of Guinness. The newspaper observed that 'regrettably the prices have changed a bit since'.[6]

During the 1980s Mulligan's was rarely left out of pubs cited in newspaper reports on increases in drink prices. Pubs that served food and those that did not became divided over a proposal to extend licensing hours. Pub owners, managers and workers objected to the change. Restaurants in pub's clothing strongly supported it.[7] Pub owners contended that there was not enough business to warrant the extension and that, if longer opening hours were introduced, there would be protracted negotiations with staff seeking extra pay and roster changes. Pubs that served food were keen to boost takings by attracting customers who had attended the theatre or late-night concert and who were looking for a meal and a drink.

Despite these changes, Mulligan's held on to its core values, particularly the ban on singing. It is, therefore, ironic that a book with its narrative set entirely in Mulligan's should have been written by one of the greatest songwriters Ireland has ever produced. *Jaysus Wept*, published in 1984, is the work of Pete St John, who wrote, among other songs, 'The Fields of Athenry', 'The Rare Ould Times' and 'The Ferryman'. The book is described on its back cover as 'a powerful, bawdy, riotously funny story of one hour in a Dublin public house – the holy hour'. It lives up to this description but it is much more.

In *Jaysus Wept*, the holy hour is described as: 'Full of nods and winks and whispers. The ticking of the grandfather clock was like a prologue to the drama. To the drink. To thinking. To rehabilitation and freedom … To letting mind [*sic*] run riot in safety.'[8] There are elements that can clearly be recognised as vintage Mulligan's, such as the Dublin/country divide. An arm wrestling match between a customer and the barman is described as: 'A thousand days of ploughing versus a thousand days of darts.'[9] The bar's intolerance of disrupting the peace is also mentioned: 'Before anyone could join in the chorus, the culchie barman said to give over – there's no singing in here – and ruined the mood.'[10] The various interactions described in the book could have occurred in any Dublin pub. However, Mulligan's offered a suitable representative setting for the holy hour antics, and enough unique material of its own to knit the narrative together.

In real life, Mulligan's holy hour was signalled by the sound of a deafening belt of a broom handle on the counters by Tommie Cusack. The aviation historian A. P. Kearns recalled that the doors would be thrown open and that, in winter, the frosty winds that chilled the bar and lounge areas were enough to empty the pub. While all on duty moved to close the premises, Tommie Cusack conveyed an urgency that few customers would or could resist. Those who remained immovable soon changed their minds as the broom was banged on the counter again, forcing pints of Guinness to jump off the bar and nearby customers to place their hands to their ringing ears.[11] Generally about six or seven customers were allowed to remain on the premises. William 'Spud' Murphy said that the holy hour was spent playing the card game, Don, in the back lounge. Customers generally got two drinks to quench their thirst and to allow Tommie Cusack to take a nap in the bar without being disturbed. Customers who asked to leave during the holy hour were forbidden to do so.[12]

The holy hour fascinated and annoyed foreign tourists, who, like the native population, found themselves without a watering hole for part of the afternoon. The actor Jer O'Leary recalled the interest that US visitors took in Irish history and, in particular, the assassination of the Minister for Justice, Kevin O'Higgins, in 1927. Many gave the view that he must have been a casualty of the bitterness that emanated from the Civil War. With tongue in cheek, O'Leary and his friends 'corrected' this observation by putting the reason for his assassination down to the fact that he had introduced the holy hour. 'Good God,' one US tourist responded, 'nothing like that ever happened during prohibition.'

The comedy inside Mulligan's contrasted with the tragedy outside. Buildings in the vicinity continued to disappear. The baths and wash-house on the corner of Tara Street and Poolbeg Street, which had been erected in May 1885 and were mentioned by Leopold Bloom in *Ulysses*, were demolished.[13] For a little over a century Mulligan's had attracted many people who had used the facilities.

The gloom in the locality and in the country generally was lifted following the appointment of Jack Charlton as manager of the Republic of Ireland soccer team in 1986. This led to an upsurge in support for the game, and consequently an upsurge in pub takings as supporters new and old flocked to their locals to cheer on the national side. The craze re-invigorated local clubs around the country, including Derry City football club, support for which had already been growing. Author and journalist Éamonn McCann recalled that the Dublin branch of the Derry City supporters club was founded in Mulligan's.[14]

When extra or replacement bar staff were needed, Mulligan's would generally contact the union, which would then send down a candidate. Not all new arrivals remained on the staff, though some who had an over-fondness for alcohol were given leeway if they worked hard or were good with customers. Paddy Kelly recalled that Tommie Cusack had a way of dealing with barmen who were too drunk to serve with him in the lounge. He would send them into the bar to work with Paddy instead. On one occasion, a tottering barman was redeployed to the bar because Tommie was too embarrassed to work with him. However, shortly afterwards, Tommie found a less exacting task for the sozzled barman – he asked him to remove a wino from the premises. This particular barman lost a great amount of verbal coherence when under the weather, a trait he found that he shared with the wino when he attempted to find words to ask him to leave. For several minutes, customers became entranced by an exchange of utterances as comprehensible as a mixture of baby-gurgling and Ancient Greek. A group of journalists nearby found they could no longer keep their counsel. One urged the barman to 'put him out'. His press colleague shouted: 'Put the f**king two of them out!'

On another occasion a woman wearing a dress with a revealing bustline pushed up to the bar one day and signalled for service. The barman, who had indulged in a similar intake of alcohol while working, arrived and asked her politely: 'Can I help you?' before adding, less politely: 'Tits off the bar, please.'[15]

The ill health from passive smoking, along with the infirmities of old age, eventually caught up with Paddy Flynn. He died in March 1987, having served in Mulligan's for fifty-two years. Christy Hynes joined the Mulligan's staff shortly afterwards. Around the same time Ger Cusack took several years out from working in the pub.[16] Christy soon found his feet, though he remembered answering the telephone on his first day and announcing to the caller, 'Cusacks'. He was quick to notice oddities, such as the insistence of locking the door linking the back lounge and bar areas: 'This was a big issue for women. There was no ladies' toilet in [the bar] and they had to walk all the way round. One or two of them actually used the gents' toilet on occasion in protest.'[17]

Regulars soon became aware of Christy's wit. A customer, who was unhappy with the price of a drink, demanded to know when 'happy hour' began. 'Whenever you leave,' Christy replied.

Another customer asked for a bottle of Blue WKD after he had noticed a poster for the vodka in the toilet: 'I said we didn't sell it. And he says to me then: "But you advertise it in a poster in the toilet."

'I said: "Yeah, but they advertise it at bus stops too but you can't buy it at bus stops, can you?" He just laughed.'[18]

Christy joined Mulligan's at a time when newspapers produced by the Irish Press group were selling well. *The Sunday Press*, in particular, was enjoying great commercial success. It had recorded sales of 432,000 in 1973 and was still outselling the *Sunday Independent* up to 1988. The *Evening Press* was wiping the floor with its main rival, the *Evening Herald*.[19] However, *The Irish Press* was in trouble and management moved to relaunch the title.

The Irish Press's format was changed from broadsheet to tabloid on 11 April 1988, amid a flurry of publicity.[20] Con Houlihan later recalled having a chat at the bar with Tommie Cusack on the morning of the relaunch, which was to be held in Mulligan's. Houlihan was not fooled by the razzmatazz. His confidence in management had evaporated. Noting the large amount of food on offer in Mulligan's – a concession granted by the owners for the event – he described the relaunch as not so much the Last Supper as the Last Breakfast.[21] As Houlihan forecast, upheavals were on the horizon in the newspaper world. The pub trade was also experiencing changes. Extensions to opening hours and the abolition of the holy hour during the week in Cork and Dublin came into force in July 1988, although the two-hour closure of pubs in Cork and Dublin on Sunday afternoons remained in place and retained its incongruous description as the holy hour. The changes provided Mulligan's and other pubs with an opportunity to increase revenues.

The following month, Tommie Cusack's son, Gary, who was eighteen years old, joined the staff on an apprentice wage of £90 a week. His father had asked him: 'Sure, come on in and stay a while.'[22] No favouritism was shown. He adjusted to the shift patterns of early lunch and early tea by cycling the forty-minute journey to and from his parents' home on the Navan Road, always being sure to arrive back on time. After one late shift, when there was no lift home available, he again made the long bicycle ride home at one o'clock in the morning. He recalled crashing into a parked car on one of his journeys as the weight of shift work and travel took its toll on him. With the help of his brother, David, he learned to drive, and bought a Ford Fiesta eighteen months after he began working in the family business.

Despite the pressures of work, Gary decided to stay: 'Every day is different, there's always something going on and it's great craic,' he said. He learned early on in his career of Mulligan's tendency to surprise. Shortly after his arrival, a barman told him that a bottle of brandy had moved of its own accord off a shelf behind the bar and into the sink without breaking. Another barman, Paddy McCormack, dealt with a curious tourist from the United States in the following manner:

Tourist: Is John Mulligan here?
McCormack: No, he's gone out.

Tourist: Where's he gone?

McCormack: He's gone to Glasnevin. [McCormack meant Glasnevin cemetery but mischievously did not explain to the tourist what he meant.]

Tourist: Do you know when he'll be back?

McCormack: No, no, no.

Tourist: When did he go out?

McCormack: 1928.[23]

Gary found, as had many others, that Mulligan's propensity for craziness extended to the vicinity. One of Mulligan's regular customers, Brian 'the Captain' O'Meara, became incensed at having fines imposed on him because he had parked his car outside the pub. O'Meara bought a tin of black paint and, with the help of another Mulligan's regular, Barney McKenna of The Dubliners, the double yellow lines directly outside Mulligan's were painted over as Peter Roche kept a look-out. However, an eagle-eyed official of Dublin Corporation spotted the break and organised for the section to be repainted. Customers observed that this repair work proved, once and for all, that parallel lines did meet, or, more correctly re-meet, and that they did so outside Mulligan's.[24]

Greater difficulties were preoccupying the journalists and printers who frequented Mulligan's, however. Problems between staff and management at *The Irish Press* manifested themselves at National Union of Journalists (NUJ) meetings held in the Joyce Room, or in animated conversations at the bar. Gary Cusack soon learned the protocol required for dealing with telephone calls to the pub. Before answering, he used to shout a typical quirky Mulligan's question: 'Is anybody not here?' to the assembled journalists and printers, who might not have wished to take calls from their employers, partners or bank managers.

Shortly after the announcement of the partnership between Irish Press Newspapers and Ingersoll Publications of New Jersey in July 1989, the editor-in-chief of *The Irish Press*, Dr Éamon de Valera, and the managing director of Ingersoll Publications, Ralph Ingersoll, paid a visit to Mulligan's. They were spotted walking down the street by one of the *Irish Press* staff. Not for the first time, the pub emptied of journalists and printers through one door as their bosses entered via the other. The two men walked around the near-deserted premises and came upon the sub-editor, Mick Cronin, who had decided not to flee. The three enjoyed a brief chat before de Valera and Ingersoll left. Cronin, who was known as Yum Yum, was famously known for breaking his fast in Mulligan's after a long drinking session by eating the raw fish he had planned to cook at home for his supper.

Cronin was known for his eccentricity. One of the *Irish Press* journalists, Dónal Byrne, recalled an incident when a newspaper vendor came into Mulligan's hoping to sell copies of the *Sunday World*, a rival to *The Sunday Press*. Cronin took the batch of newspapers and began tearing them up one by one in front of the vendor.

These unexpected scenarios meant that Mulligan's barmen required the back-up of a sixth sense or, at least, a supernatural aptitude to think on their feet to avert trouble. Its owners had refined their recruitment methods so as to appoint employees who would have the necessary skills to deal with the Mulligan's maze. This refinement involved a weighing up of the interviewee by observation more than by questioning. Billy 'Swiss' Phelan recalled the interview he underwent with Con Cusack in 1989:

> *Con Cusack:* Do you follow the GAA?
>
> *Billy Phelan:* I do. I do, Con.
>
> *Cusack:* And what county are you from?
>
> *Billy:* I'm from Laois.
>
> *Cusack:* Well I'm from Cavan so we'll make this interview fairly short. Would you be able to start next Saturday?

Billy began work as arranged. He said that Tommie Cusack, who had been undergoing an operation, returned to work a few weeks later:

> Tommie looked in behind the counter. He said, 'Who's yer man? Who took him on?' And somebody said, 'Con'. He let [out] a grunt and that was it.

Billy said that he got on very well with both Con and Tommie: 'They never brought the staff into any of their own problems.' He also found he had an immediate affinity with the pub:

I love Mulligan's. I loved it from day one. Because of the clientèle and the mix. The customers seem to know that bad behaviour won't be tolerated and that type of customer doesn't appear. You don't have to be refusing every second one that comes in.

Billy enjoyed 'the cross-section of customers, getting the chance to meet different people all the time, discussing the history of the pub, what films were made here, or just examining the news'.[25] Among the films under discussion at the time was *My Left Foot*, based on the book by Christy Brown. The film, directed by Jim Sheridan, won Oscars for best actor in a leading role (Daniel Day-Lewis) and best actress in a supporting role (Brenda Fricker). A set that was a replica of Mulligan's bar was used for scenes in the film.

Billy has honoured the tradition in Mulligan's, where the unexpected was not limited to the customer's side of the counter:

Once a regular complained that there was something wrong with his pint. Billy examined the Guinness and caressed it before downing the drink. 'There's nothing wrong with that pint,' he said, putting the empty glass back on the counter.[26]

He also became a close friend of Con Houlihan, accompanying him to matches and regularly finding remarks he had made appearing with a suitable credit in Houlihan's *Evening Press* column.

The waves of change that had followed the French Revolution in 1789 caused a ripple in Mulligan's 200 years later. The folk singer Liam Clancy was in Mulligan's entertaining members of the French diplomatic corps in connection with a film being screened to mark the bicentenary. Tommie Cusack immediately ordered Clancy to obey the house rule and stop singing. Customers attempted in vain to explain that the National Concert Hall was charging £12 to anyone who wanted to hear Clancy sing. Paddy Kelly recalled that one customer asked Tommie did he not know who he was, but Tommie's mind was fixed: 'I don't give a f**k who he is. There's no singing here.'[27] During his career with the Clancy Brothers and later with Tommy Makem, Clancy had filled the largest concert halls on tours around the world. However, despite this reputation, he was obliged to bend to the Mulligan's rule.[28]

11

PRESS CLOSES

The participation of the Republic of Ireland's soccer team in the World Cup (Italia '90) brought an unprecedented level of energy and optimism to the mood of the country. Mulligan's thrived as supporters squeezed their way into all corners of the premises to watch the national team's encounters with England, Egypt and the Netherlands (Ireland drew with all of them), its victory over Romania on penalties, and its eventual defeat against the home side in the quarter-finals. (It is widely thought by those who have not been to Mulligan's that the pub has never had a television. In fact, a photograph dating from 1967 shows a television in the back lounge.)

The rainbow of good humour generated by Italia '90 was dulled in Mulligan's by renewed rows between management and staff at Irish Press Newspapers that dragged on for weeks. It was widely believed, both inside and outside the offices at Burgh Quay, that the company's three titles were facing extinction. Matters came to a head on 22 July 1990. Journalists, printers and office staff entered and exited Mulligan's as negotiations began between the NUJ and management representatives. Eventually, a settlement was reached:

After the [NUJ] chapel meeting, the staff again spilled out to the neighbouring bars and cafés. It wasn't quite like All-Ireland final day in Mulligan's but it was close. 'It's been a great Sunday,' said proprietor Con Cusack. 'When are ye going to be sacked again? Can ye be sacked every Sunday?'[1]

Four months later, a promotional campaign for *The Sunday Press* began. Advertisements asserted that: 'Even after the pubs close on Saturday night, you'll still find our journalists putting the finishing touches to the latest news reports for the final edition.' The headline to the advertisement ran: 'You won't find them in Mulligan's of Poolbeg Street on Saturday night.'[2]

In December 1990 supporters of the newly installed President Mary Robinson conducted their celebrations in Dublin in the Barley Mow pub, Francis Street, moving on for speeches and lunch to Kitty O'Shea's, Grand Canal Street, before completing their festivities with evening drinks at Mulligan's.[3]

Customers could generally find well-known people in the pub on any day of the week. The Hollywood actor, Brian Dennehy, found time to relax there between performances at the Abbey Theatre in Eugene O'Neill's play *The Iceman Cometh*. The play had an approximate running time of four hours and forty-five minutes. One night, Paddy Kelly served Dennehy and a friend, who was wearing a hat. Customers needed no help from some journalists present to recognise the imposing presence of Dennehy. However, they did require the eagle eye of one journalist, who was able to reveal the identity of Dennehy's mysterious companion. When Paddy returned home that night he was happy to tell his wife that one of her favourite film actors, Kevin Costner, had been in Mulligan's.[4]

Thomas Keneally, who won the Booker Prize in 1982 for *Schindler's Ark,* used Mulligan's to announce, while savouring a pint of Guinness, that he was writing a book about Ireland.[5] Seamus Heaney often found solace in Mulligan's, both before and after he received the Nobel Prize for Literature in 1995. On hearing of Heaney's death, John Menaghan, a poet and professor of English at Loyola Marymount University, Los Angeles, California, recalled a poignant moment involving himself and Heaney in the early 1990s:

> I found myself in Mulligan's, a pub near the Trinity College campus that has a reputation for attracting writers and journalists. It was a quiet night, and I sat alone at one end of the bar, waiting for my pint of Guinness to settle before taking a sip. While waiting, I cast my eyes around the room, only to discover, sitting at the opposite end of the bar, the great Seamus Heaney. To my further surprise, he was also alone. Two opposite impulses arose in me. One was the obvious one, that I should seize this chance to slide down the bar and have a chat with him. The other was to leave him alone, because it occurred to me that there must be very few times in recent years when he'd been able to have a quiet pint in a pub, without being besieged by people wanting to be able to say they'd had a personal encounter with Seamus Heaney. And no one else in the pub

was bothering him, so why should I? In the end, I left him alone, and a part of me always regretted it. Because – although, over the years, I saw him read numerous times and, even at one reading, went up to introduce myself and thank him for a great reading – I felt I had missed my chance to get to know him in the more relaxed setting of the pub, and perhaps even become friends. Yet another part of me still thinks I might have done the right thing to leave him alone that night and let him enjoy his own company. And today, when I heard he was gone, it was seeing him alone at the end of the bar in Mulligan's, rather than giving a reading in any number of venues large and small, that came back to me most powerfully, and made me feel a wordless connection with this great master of language who was, in that time and place, just another Irishman sitting in a pub, enjoying his quiet pint.[6]

Not all famous people found Mulligan's a pleasant experience, however. When the ballet dancer Wayne Sleep arrived on the premises he did a pirouette and frolicked up and down the bar in front of a perplexed and wary Gary Cusack, who was on duty. Both he and his fellow-worker Seán Keegan attempted to assess the sobriety of Sleep and his entourage. When the dancer had completed his routine he ordered a Jameson whiskey, emphasising the brand's three syllables with equal stress. Gary Cusack concluded his assessment and, in true Mulligan's tradition, expressed his response concisely: 'Good luck.' Sleep understood the direction to leave, and he and his troupe departed.[7]

A group of people who were born deaf or who had become deaf in later life found Mulligan's a more welcoming spot than Sleep. In May 1991 they began meeting there on Sunday nights and continue to do so. One of their number, Martin Mannion, said that communicating with the barmen had not been a problem: 'They know the signs for Guinness, Heineken, pint and half glass. They even know the sign for bullshit.' Another member of the group claims never to have experienced a hangover from drinking Guinness in Mulligan's, despite having good reason to do so.[8]

Writing in the *Irish Independent*, Justine McCarthy described a 'bookish pub crawl' she undertook in June 1991 in the company of poets and actors. Among them was the poet Gabriel Rosenstock, then chairman of Poetry Ireland, who questioned if anyone had noticed that 'none of the so-called literary pubs has a book stand'. He also complained about how pubs had changed:

> Dublin pubs have been yuppified beyond belief. If any of us walked into the majority of these yuppie pubs I don't think they would recognise us as writers and, secondly, if they did, I don't think they would have much respect for us.

Mulligan's was one of the stops on the pub crawl. McCarthy reported that 'The dour barman asked nobody in particular and in utter disdain: "Where did all these yuppies come from?"'[9]

The Hollywood actress Julia Roberts and the actor Jason

Patric celebrated Bloomsday on 16 June 1991 by taking a stroll around Dublin that included a visit to Mulligan's. The barman on duty, Christy Hynes, observed that, despite their fame, the couple were left alone and no autograph hunters sought to disturb their private excursion.[10]

Another Hollywood film actor, Sean Penn, was not so lucky when he arrived at the pub with the film director Jim Sheridan and friends. Shortly after the party had taken a seat at the table in the back lounge closest to the entry door, the *Irish Press* photographer, Aidan O'Keeffe swooped:

The renowned hell-raiser attempted to hide his face from the approaching photographer. Late night drinkers in the lounge looked on bemused as the pressman was blocked by a barman [Gary Cusack] and jostled by the actor's entourage.

'We can do a deal if you're interested,' Penn told Aidan O'Keeffe menacingly. 'You can take a picture of me now, if we can take it outside.'

At closing time, Penn attempted to avoid further exposure by entering the bar section of the premises by a side door and emerging unexpectedly at the front, his jacket pulled over his head.

He then jumped into a car, which was driven off by a woman, with Sheridan and another man on board, and Penn shielding his face in the rear seat.

Despite Penn's attempts to avoid the press, the intrepid O'Keeffe got his picture.[11]

A day after *The Irish Press* published the photograph, Penn was interviewed by a reporter from the newspaper, who noted that he appeared 'a little the worse for wear' having spent the previous evening in various pubs in Dublin. Despite the incident in Mulligan's, he said he had enjoyed his night on the town.[12]

At around that time, Gary Cusack recorded a series of incidents on the premises that were more curious than the events surrounding Penn's visit. For a brief period in the early 1990s Gary made the upstairs of No. 8 Poolbeg Street his home. This decision led to him experiencing an unexplained phenomenon on the premises. During several nights he heard what he thought was the sound of someone walking up and down the floor of the top room. He went to investigate the noise on one occasion, but could not find the source of it.[13]

Other strange incidents followed. Tommie's son Brian began working alongside his brothers Gary and Ger when he was studying for a law degree. Of the many curious incidents to have been recorded in Mulligan's, Brian was to witness one of the most strange. He and Gary were working in the front lounge bar when Gary felt and heard a knock from beneath the cellar hatch on which they were both standing. They knew there was no one in the cellar. Gary turned to Brian to ask him if he had noticed anything. He had heard and felt the same rap from the hatch. They both waited a while, afraid to check the source of the noise as they laughed nervously. Eventually, Gary opened the hatch and checked the cellar. There was no one there.[14]

Their colleague, Christy Hynes, related another unexplained phenomenon that happened in the early 1990s, along with two other instances:

> I was downstairs ... at the ice-machine ... pouring stuff [beer slops] down the drains and I had two buckets of it. I had one bucket down beside me and I turned around to get it and it was gone and nobody had passed me, nobody could physically pass you. I looked down and it was down at the end of the cellar. I didn't hang around then. I came back up and left it there.
>
> On another occasion, I was doing the same thing and I was at the ice machine – that's where the drain is, you see – and I felt kind as if there was somebody watching me. So I turned around and I looked down and there was a man sitting on a keg down at the end of the cellar. He wasn't even looking at me. He was looking straight ahead as if he was minding his own business. I just felt cold. That was it really. I didn't feel afraid or anything but I wouldn't like to be on my own when it happened.
>
> The other occasion was actually upstairs. It was after work and we were sitting down and I was in the lounge. I was having a Coke and someone walked by in the bar and looked over at me. I said to somebody, I can't remember who was with me at the time: 'There's somebody in the bar.' And there was nobody else on the premises at all. But he actually stopped in the doorway and looked over at me. It was definitely a man. I thought it was a customer. I actually went around and there was no one on the premises.[15]

About ten years after this, another barman, Danny Tracey, was enjoying a drink after closing time in the front lounge when he too looked through the entrance to the front bar and saw a male figure passing by. His drinking companion at the bar also saw the figure. But again, there was no one to be found in the bar area. This was the second recorded instance of an unexplained phenomenon in Mulligan's being witnessed by two people simultaneously, the other being when Gary and Brian Cusack heard the knock from the cellar hatch in the front lounge.

During the 1990s Mulligan's attracted politicians from both sides of the political divide in Northern Ireland. The decade saw a coming together of politicians such as US President Bill Clinton, British Prime Ministers John Major and Tony Blair, and Taoisigh Albert Reynolds and Bertie Ahern, in the quest for peace. Two of the most visionary representatives in this movement were loyalists David Ervine and Billy Hutchinson of the Progressive Unionist Party. Both drank in Mulligan's. In fact, Ervine cited McDaid's, Harry Street, Dublin, and Mulligan's as being among his favourite pubs.[16]

On the other side of the political spectrum was Gerry O'Hare, a former public relations officer for the republican movement in Belfast, who later became a journalist with the Irish Press group and was a regular in Mulligan's. Gary Cusack recalled a conversation he had with O'Hare in 1993, during which mention was made of the escape of IRA internees by helicopter from Mountjoy Prison in Dublin exactly twenty years earlier. When asked why he was looking so happy, O'Hare replied that he was celebrating the anniversary of the breakout:

'Were you covering it?'

'Covering it?' questioned O'Hare. 'I was in it.'[17]

O'Hare was one of many journalists who frequented Mulligan's. Indeed, the regular presence of journalists on the premises greatly helped to ensure that Mulligan's was rarely omitted from pub reviews because they were generally written by its most loyal customers. However, not all reviews raved about the premises. The *Irish Independent* noted: 'Easy access but very crowded, guide dogs permitted.'[18] The same newspaper reported that the president of Wang Laboratories, Richard Miller, 'was introduced to the joys of stout in Mulligan's' during a visit to inspect the company's operation in Ireland. The journalist added: 'Whether it was that experience, or the fact that Wang Ireland was able to report a record year, Mr Miller has decided to return for a family holiday.'[19] Writing in *The Irish Press*, Jim McNeill told readers that sipping a pint of shandy in Mulligan's at Sunday lunchtime was 'as civilised a way as any to start off the week'.[20] In a review of television sports coverage of the Barcelona Olympics, Karl Johnston was less than impressed by a judo match between a British competitor and his French opponent: 'Yes I know judo is skilful but for grace and agility you'd see better than this in the back bar of Mulligan's of Poolbeg Street any night of the week.'[21]

The Boston Globe told readers that the front door of Mulligan's sticks, especially after rain, but that regulars know enough to tug hard: 'If a good yank is enough to keep away a bad yank – that is, a loud, obnoxious, camera-toting, plaid-pants-wearing American who wants to buy the house a round – well, then God bless.' Newcomers, the review went on, were easy to spot: 'They stare, either enthralled or appalled, at the surroundings.'[22]

Barry McCall of the *Irish Independent*, accompanied Grace Dolan from Massachusetts around Dublin to see how tourist-friendly the city was. They were unhappy with the lack of information given to them until they arrived at Mulligan's:

> Grace sat at the bar and ordered her drink, spilling a pile of change out on the counter, telling the barman [Christy Hynes] that she didn't understand the money. This was the ideal opportunity to get ripped off – and it didn't happen. [Christy] patiently went through all the change, told her what the different coins were and took the exact money for [the] drink.
>
> She then asked him for his advice on places to go and things to do. He proved to have an encyclopaedic knowledge of places and things of interest to tourists and was only too willing to share it. His advice ranged from walks along the Wicklow coast to a variety of exhibitions and so on. He also admitted that he hadn't been to a lot of these places himself but had heard they were very good.
>
> Alongside this general advice, he gave clear and accurate directions on getting to the places, including public transport facilities. He literally took Grace under his wing. When another customer came in he would serve them quickly and politely and immediately return to his counselling session with Grace.

I have to admit that even I was impressed with this level of service and courtesy.[23]

An indication of how Mulligan's had penetrated the psyche of the general public is evident in the film *Hear My Song*, released in 1991, which revolved around the colourful life of the Irish tenor Josef Locke. The *Irish Times* film critic, Michael Dwyer, described how the director had used the pub:

> When the film moves from Liverpool to Dublin, one of the first shots of the city is outside Mulligan's pub as a priest in a soutane walks by. This, we can assume, is an establishing shot in the same way as a red bus tells us we're in London or a shot of the Eiffel Tower signals Paris as a setting.[24]

As Ger Cusack prepared to return to Mulligan's in 1993 following a seven-year absence, the pub and his father, Tommie, were holding their reputation for throwing surprises. The *Irish Press* television critic, Declan Lynch, was enjoying a couple of after-work drinks in Mulligan's when he was approached by a woman looking for extras for Jim Sheridan's film *In the Name of the Father*. Lynch spent a day on the set with the lead actor, Daniel Day-Lewis.[25]

Three days before the Soccer World Cup qualifier between the Republic of Ireland and Lithuania in September 1993, three of Ireland's top players (past and present) – Niall Quinn, Denis Irwin and Kevin Moran – were spotted in Mulligan's having a drink. However, it was not the Lithuanian match they were concerned with: 'the three were buzzing with excitement about the hurling All-Ireland between Kilkenny and Galway that they had seen in Croke Park earlier'.[26]

Also in 1993, the government passed all stages of the Family Planning (Amendment) Bill, which allowed condoms to be bought in shops and from vending machines. A saleswoman entered Mulligan's shortly afterwards and asked Tommie Cusack would he be interested in installing a condom machine: 'No,' said Tommie, 'our lads go bareback or not at all – we'll get draught cider in first.'[27]

Blue signs with white lettering were placed in the bar and lounge areas in the early 1990s: 'PLEASE USE MOBILE PHONES OUTSIDE PREMISES'. Barman Christy Hynes said the signs were brought in by a customer as a joke when mobile phones were the size of bricks. Since its inception, this rule has rarely, if ever, been enforced.

While Irish coffees are served in Mulligan's, sometimes – because of hectic service or the mood of a barman – the customer is directed elsewhere, as Con Houlihan noted:

> Two couples in their forties came in and asked for Irish coffee. Tommie directed them to the White Horse around the corner. They came back with four cups and one of the women said: 'We promised our friends back in Ohio that we would drink Irish coffee in Mulligan's.'[28]

In 1994 Con Houlihan, who was in Cheltenham to report on the racing festival, had a bad fall. It happened on Tuesday

15 March as he rushed to get an evening train back to Birmingham. A bellboy helped him up to his hotel room on a luggage cart, and from the hotel Houlihan rang his partner or, as he liked to call her, his 'friend girl', Harriet Duffin, in Dublin:

> Con announced impassively that he might just give the Wednesday card a miss and return to his station on Gold Cup day [Thursday].
>
> As soon as he hung up, she rang reception. 'Can you please get a doctor for the man in room …' That evening, Con would be operated on in a Birmingham hospital. The fall had broken his hip.
>
> It was a mishap that would carry repercussions for the rest of his life. Four times he was operated on for hip replacements, four times the procedure failed. It may have been a consequence of his giant frame, but the failures pitched Con into a state of almost constant pain.[29]

The Republic of Ireland's qualification for a second successive soccer World Cup coincided with a strike by barmen over pay, pensions and improved wages for staff involved in pub catering. The start of the strike coincided with the Republic of Ireland's first game against Italy at Giants Stadium in East Rutherford, New Jersey, on 18 June 1994.

The strike was the lead story on the front page of the early edition of *The Sunday Press*, which also featured a picture of three Mulligan's barmen – Mick McGovern, Billy Phelan and Christy Hynes – picketing outside the pub. Then, in New Jersey, Ray Houghton scored a goal that resulted in victory for his team. In a later edition, the front page was given over almost entirely to the Republic of Ireland's win; a photograph of Houghton replaced the one of Mulligan's and the lead story was swapped for a report on the team's triumph over Italy.[30] The barmen's strike ended after four days, when they voted to accept settlement terms.[31]

The strike did not damage relations between management and staff at Mulligan's. In fact, Tommie Cusack encouraged the barmen to fight for better terms.[32] However, relations between Tommie and his family did become strained when he began trying to recruit some of them to help out with the harvest on his farm in County Cavan. He found that none of them was available to cover for him in the bar while he dealt with the harvest. As a result, he had to break his farm work and return to Mulligan's. He was not in the best of moods when he arrived for work in the pub on 1 September 1994. However, it all soon changed when he was greeted by his wife, Evelyn, his children, friends and customers for a surprise party sponsored by Guinness and marking his fiftieth year in Mulligan's. *The Irish Press* described him as the city's best-known barman and reported that, for once, he was perched on the right side of the counter sipping his favourite tipple – a bottle of Guinness. He said he had no regrets at having stuck to the one job and missing out on the rest of life:

All life has been in this bar. The famous and infamous. Mulligan's attracted them all, characters you wouldn't believe.

But you know the best characters were the dockers; Jockser Gibbs and Butterkrust, Mick Byrne. They'd have you laughing till you cried with their sayings and views of life.

But when it came to the speechmaking last night, Tommie had just one thing to say, an old saying he picked up on his first night's service – 'Now gentlemen, please'.[33]

The 'Night Town' reporter on *The Irish Press*, Myles McEntee, was delighted to hear that Tommie's wife, Evelyn, was in Mulligan's to celebrate the event.[34] He decided to approach her and found that she had as enchanting a way with conversation as her husband. He introduced himself by saying he was Myles from the *Press*. She mistook his meaning and reassured him that the *Press* was only next door.[35]

Fears for the future of the Irish Press group of newspapers had been raised on so many occasions that people outside no longer took them seriously, so it came as a shock to most when the papers ceased publication in May 1995 following protracted rows between workers and management. This resulted in 640 people losing their jobs. Reporters, sub-editors, columnists and former executives flocked to Mulligan's, where they attempted to drown their sorrows.

The former *Irish Times* journalist, Frank Kilfeather, said that journalists in all other newspapers were very sad to see *The Irish Press* cease publication. He gave his opinion of how the newspaper and its journalists were viewed by their rivals:

It had an enviable record for producing all the hard news, rarely missed a story, and what you read was tightly and factually written. It was the complete newspaper, with emphasis on the news, no waffle or pretentious pontificating. If you wanted the news you bought the *Press*. They covered the country like a Hoover. It was a great paper to train on. You had to have all of the facts and your copy had to be accurately written. There were never any loose ends. It was a real newsman's paper.[36]

Over time, the redundancy money ran out and former Press employees got jobs elsewhere, many of them having retrained for other careers. The crowds that had once filled Mulligan's were no more. Never again would the rumble of the presses from Burgh Quay be heard in Mulligan's, as they had been for more than sixty years. The journalist, Vincent Reddin, recalled a statement Tommie Cusack made shortly after the closure of the Irish Press group: 'That's it now, Reddin, we're finished. That's the end of it now.'[37]

12

A New Century

The owners and staff of Mulligan's felt a great deal of sadness at the closure of the Irish Press group of newspapers, for two reasons. The first was the obvious loss of revenue that threatened the business and consequently their livelihoods. The second was the departure over time of many of their regular customers who had become either friends or institutions in their own right.

Some Irish Press workers barricaded themselves inside the Burgh Quay offices. Former staff brought out the *Xpress* newspaper. It included exclusive interviews with U2 and Stephen Rea, who was appearing in the film *Michael Collins*, and a column by Jack Charlton for which he took no fee. Con Houlihan regularly met one of the *Xpress* journalists, Liam Mackey, in Mulligan's to give him his handwritten copy for the publication.[1] Houlihan also sold the newspaper on O'Connell Bridge and described his new job in the context of the Arthur Miller play *Death of a Salesman*. However, the publication folded, putting a full stop to the long history of publishing by the Irish Press group of newspapers. Whether the grand old pub of Poolbeg Street would survive such a devastating blow, against Tommie Cusack's forecast, remained to be seen.

The closure of the Press newspapers coincided with the start of what was to become known as the Celtic Tiger, when the Republic of Ireland's economy experienced a five-year period of rapid growth and a subsequent property bubble that ended in the country crashing to its knees in 2008. In Mulligan's the crumpled hacks, ink-stained case-room staff and exotic interviewees of the Irish Press group gave way to portly young men with Crombie coats and busy mobile phones.

Mulligan's decided to leave a permanent reminder on the premises of the Irish Press group in the form of a plaque to Con Houlihan, which was erected on a wall in the front lounge. Underneath a monochrome photograph of him with his trademark brandy and milk was placed a Brendan Kennelly poem, 'The Big Man', and a dedication by John B. Keane.

The colour and buzz brought to Mulligan's by its unofficial public relations officer, Peter Roche, helped to ease the dim mood that hung over the staff and remaining customers alike on the loss of the Press newspapers. On the instruction of the former *Irish Times* journalist and Mulligan's diehard, Tomás Ó Duinn, Roche bought a blackboard and chalk, to be used for Irish language lessons in the Joyce Room. The enthusiasm shown by the more senior Mulligan's customers for this project diminished shortly after the first lesson. Roche soon found himself to be Ó Duinn's sole remaining pupil and was pleasantly surprised when his teacher suggested at the start of the lesson: 'I think we might go out and have a pint.'

'I think we might,' Roche replied.[2]

In 1995 Peter Roche took charge of the many telephone calls to Mulligan's on St Patrick's Day, a task he had undertaken before this and which he continues to undertake. The pub is the default destination for many media outlets in Australia, Britain and the United States, where it has become well known over its long history. John Kelly, the former reporter and features writer for the Irish Press group, estimated that, while presiding over his favoured corner, Roche took about thirty calls from various media outlets, most of them from the United States. In his column in *The Irish Echo*, Kelly also related that in August 1995 Roche was waiting for a reply from the White House to an invitation he had sent to President Bill Clinton to visit Mulligan's.[3] The US president did indeed enjoy a pint of Guinness during his visit to Dublin, but in Cassidy's pub in Camden Street, and not in Mulligan's.

The Mulligan's Christmas draw, organised by Peter Roche, celebrated its twenty-first year in 1995. The anniversary was marked by the attendance of the lord mayor of Dublin, Seán 'Dublin Bay' Loftus, who fulfilled the engagement despite having a heavy cold.[4]

The following year, Paddy Kelly retired from Mulligan's, having worked there for twelve years. He said he liked the pub because there was not the tension between management and staff that he had found in other establishments:

Mulligan's allowed you to do your own thing, maybe too much

for their own good. It was an experience, I'd hated to have missed it. I certainly met the loveliest of people in there and that's the amazing thing about it too; the loveliest people go into it.[5]

The closure of Sam Greer's saddlers in 1998 took away another long-established business from Poolbeg Street. The shop had provided saddles for horses used by the Dublin Metropolitan Police before the establishment of the Irish Free State and came full circle by doing similar work for the Garda Mounted Unit, which was established the year that Greer's shop closed. The closure of the saddlers did not go unnoticed. The horses bearing Greer's saddles were brought down to Poolbeg Street to be photographed. With the help of his rider, one of the horses poked its head into the door of the bar area of Mulligan's but went no further.[6]

Con Houlihan, despite enduring continuing pain from failed hip operations, was carving out a new career with the *Sunday World*. Similar to his *Evening Press* column, he devoted space to his friends to wish them well or to commiserate with them. One of his most heartfelt tributes was to Mick McGovern, who died in 1998. He had worked as a barman in Mulligan's for twenty-seven years. Houlihan accorded McGovern an honour that was all the greater for the experience of pubs that Houlihan could draw on: 'It is fair to say that there was no more popular barman in Dublin.'[7]

Mulligan's lost another of its pillars later in the year, this time through retirement. Con Cusack decided to hang up his white apron after almost half a century of service. His friend and long-time customer, Con Houlihan, said Con Cusack liked to give the impression that he was hard and wise in the ways of the world, which he was, but he also said he cared about people: 'There is no greater virtue.'[8] Houlihan presented Cusack with a photograph of himself standing beside Mulligan's grandfather clock, and the picture was hung in the front room of the Cusacks' home in Clontarf. Con sold his share in the pub to his brother, Tommie, and nephews, Gary and Ger.[9] Christy Hynes was on duty the day the deal was concluded:

> I never saw them having a cross word with each other. They never spoke bad of each other either. I remember the time Con sold up his share, he came in and Tommie went down and served him a drink. I said to Tommie, 'Con is in there he's looking for a drink,' and Tommie said, 'Oh, I'll go in and serve him.' They went down and had a chat in the front bar.[10]

A year later Gary Cusack remarked in an interview with the *Irish Independent* that the longevity of service such as that given by his uncle Con and McGovern was becoming a mark of the past. He also listed the requisite talents of a Mulligan's barman: honesty, loyalty and an ability to get on with the customers.[11]

Seven months into the twenty-first century, the government passed a law that extended pub opening hours on Thursdays, Fridays and Saturdays and abolished the two-hour closure on Sunday afternoons.[12] The disappearance of the 'holy hour' was celebrated by drinkers and publicans alike, who had lived under the shadow of what they saw as a disruption to their working day and the customers' enjoyment of a Sunday afternoon drink.

The first years of the new century saw a rise in the number of celebrities visiting the pub, among them the stage magician Paul Daniels, and his wife, Debbie McGee. The former Portuguese soccer international Eusebio signed a photograph of himself for Ger Cusack, which was placed on the wall behind the front lounge counter. The Oscar-winning actor Ralph Fiennes and the actress Amanda Barrie, who played Alma Sedgewick (later Baldwin) in the British soap opera *Coronation Street*, were among the actors who visited the pub.[13]

In 2001 Tommie Cusack's son, Ger, introduced his thirteen-year-old son, Darran, to working in Mulligan's, undertaking cellar work and collecting glasses. This continued a 200-year-old tradition of family members doing their apprenticeship in the business.[14]

Mulligan's extended its connection with the silver screen and small screen, from serving those appearing on them to being used as a set for national and international television and film productions. The pub was used as the local in the RTÉ television series *Bachelors Walk*, a comedy drama about three single men living in a house in Dublin. John Carney, who co-wrote and co-directed the series, explained why the pub was chosen as a location:

I had been looking for years at ways and formats of photograph-
ing Dublin. We were trying to get a sense of the real city. Not the
city of the Globe Bar and Rí-Rá, but the unofficial, independent
city. That's why the characters drink in the old-style Mulligan's of
Poolbeg Street and there is hardly a cappuccino bar to be seen.[15]

After the programme was broadcast, Mulligan's barman
Danny Tracey noticed a slight change in the type of customer
frequenting the pub: 'There was a little difference in the
clientèle, more the student type or young women, essentially
the audience which the programme appealed to. It put us on
the map for people calling in.'[16]

The pub was also used for interior scenes in the ITV
drama series *Foyle's War*. Gary Cusack made a brief appearance
behind the bar in the 2003 black comedy film *Dead Bodies*.
A documentary on the life of Con Houlihan, *Waiting for
Houlihan*, which featured him being served brandy and milk
and chatting about sport with barman Paddy Kelly, was
broadcast on RTÉ in 2004.

However, the pub's relationship with the world of the
performing arts – which had already seen fractious encounters
with Wayne Sleep and Sean Penn – was not always good-
tempered. Early in 2003 Peter O'Toole went to the pub with a
friend. A barman refused to serve O'Toole, having formed an
impression that the actor had already had too much to drink.
When Billy Phelan returned to work after a break, the actor
Paul Bennett 'reared up' on him about the incident.[17] A few
months later O'Toole was presented with an honorary Oscar at

the Academy Awards in Los Angeles. Customers in Mulligan's commented at the time that O'Toole was not only invited but lauded at an event which many would have given their right arm to attend, but he could not get served in Mulligan's.

A smoking ban in workplaces came into force in Ireland on 29 March 2004. Two days beforehand, the Minister for Health, Micheál Martin, publicised the restriction at an event in Mulligan's.

On Christmas Eve 2004, Tommie Cusack fell ill and was admitted to hospital. Over the next two years daily visits by his family members were punctuated by others from his many friends and customers. He died on 28 March 2006, aged seventy-eight. At his funeral, anecdotes were exchanged about him. Danny Tracey recalled Tommie's generosity: 'He would always send down a tray of drinks if we happened to meet outside Mulligan's, and dare anyone try to send a drink back to him.'[18] Tommie's love of Rowntree's fruit gums was also brought up, as was his habitual sweeping of the Navan Road. This exercise incorporated the footpaths of neighbours' houses and often involved an unhurried chat with them, an aspect of his character that came from his rural background. Con Houlihan paid a final tribute to his friend:

He had a great life, he was fulfilled. And he left his ship in good family hands. I suppose you could call it the Cusack Stand.[19]

The pub passed into the hands of Tommie's sons, Gary and Ger, at a time when confidence in business in Ireland was soaring. Stuart Brechin and Gavin Watchorn set up the Brechin Watchorn wine chain. Watchorn said their business plan was largely written on the backs of beer mats at Mulligan's and the Dockers pub, on Sir John Rogerson's Quay, because 'they were our business development offices'.[20]

In 2006 the Dublin Theatre Festival celebrated its fiftieth year. David Soul joined the cast of *The Exonerated* at the Liberty Hall Theatre, located on the other side of the River Liffey from where Mulligan's is situated. The play relates the stories of six innocent survivors of death row. Soul found a way to relax after intense performances of such serious subject matter by crossing the bridge over the Liffey, as Billy Phelan recalled:

> He was in Mulligan's nearly every night for the week. He loved a pint of Guinness. I remember the last thing he said to me before he left. He stood in the middle of the pub and let out a roar: 'Billy, that's the best f**king pint of Guinness I've ever drunk in my life.'[21]

In 2007 Darran Cusack won the DIT Cocktail Challenge, sponsored by Irish Distillers Pernod Ricard; a total of eighty competitors took part. Darran also took top honours in the competition the following year.[22] His success in these competitions and the relative ease with which he adapted to working in the bar trade came not only from what he had learned from his family but also because he is greatly attracted to the dynamics of the trade:

There's not a day that I would wake up and say: 'Oh, I don't want to come in here again.' I've never given out about coming into work here. If I didn't enjoy it I wouldn't be doing it. It's like anything in life, you'll enjoy doing it and stick with it.[23]

However, the good times eventually came to an end. When the Irish economy crashed in 2008, threatening question marks appeared over the future of many businesses, including Mulligan's. The years following the crash brought an unusual amount of focus on Mulligan's from writers and television producers. Frank McCourt, who wrote the best-selling autobiography *Angela's Ashes*, included the pub in a US television documentary *Historic Pubs of Dublin*, which he presented. McCourt described Mulligan's as 'an institution, a classic, a masterpiece', and observed: 'This pub is a tabernacle to the serious drinker; no food served here. Sometimes when you focus on just one thing you become really good at it.'[24] Thomas Kennedy published two thriller novels revolving around the Joyce Room in Mulligan's.[25] Bill Barich gave an assessment of Mulligan's in his book on tradition, change and the fate of the Irish pub in *A Pint of Plain*. Barich recounted: 'How many times had a callow lad slaving for the minimum wage brought me an unsatisfactory Guinness? Too many to count, in fact, although you couldn't blame the rookie, because he'd never been trained except in the most basic skills.'[26] Barich approached Mulligan's with apprehension:

So little light filtered through the streaked windows I felt as if

I'd stumbled into an old country manor only recently opened to the air again after the death of its owner ... I recognised the fellow behind the bar from the website – Christy [Hynes], who wore a broad, inviting grin and had the sturdy frame of a baseball catcher ... I took a seat at a long, hard refectory table. As the seconds ticked by, I was eager to see if the Guinness Christy poured would match its reputation.

Barich then explained what happened when the pint arrived:

The stout did not froth, bubble, or threaten to erupt, nor did a ripple run through it anywhere. Instead it radiated a sense of calm, if such a thing were possible, and Christy delivered it precisely when the beer had completed its gyrations and fully settled. The pint was picture-perfect. A quarter inch of foam topped the black stuff with its slight ruby tinge, and the stout was cool, not ice-cold, and crisp and very clean on the palate. Could Christy perform the same trick twice? I put the challenge to him, and he accepted. His second pint duplicated the first in every detail, a feat worthy of a citation in, well, the *Guinness Book of World Records*.[27]

These mentions helped to publicise the Mulligan's brand name. So too did the many times Mulligan's was featured on television channels around the world, as file pictures of the pub were inserted into news reports of the impact of the economic crisis in Ireland. Despite this, the recession took its toll on Mulligan's and two barmen were let go.

Many factors had contributed to the depletion of Mulligan's clientèle since the start of the new century, including the smoking ban, the change in the culture of people's drinking habits, the financial crash and the reduction in the number of tourists, particularly from the United States, following the terrorist attacks of 11 September 2001.

One US tourist, who continued to make infrequent trips to Ireland and to Mulligan's, was Billy Brooks Carr, from Texas. His untimely death on 18 August 2011 did not stop his visits, however. Some of his ashes were scattered at hole fourteen at the Clear Creek golf course, Houston, where he and his brothers had all had holes-in-one, and portions were deposited in a selection of the finest Irish pubs in Houston, Texas. Eight months later, one of his closest friends, Charles 'Doc' Dougherty, was setting off for a trip to Dublin when he asked Billy's brother, Mike, if he could do anything for him or for Billy's twin, Dave:

We told him we would give him some of Billy's ashes and asked him to go to John Mulligan's, have a drink with Billy and spread his ashes outside the pub after the drink. Noel [Hawkins] was the bartender when Doc ordered two pints of Guinness. As Noel was topping off the first pint, he asked Doc if he wanted to wait on his friend to top off the second pint. Doc then pulled out Billy's ashes and asked Noel to finish building it, that his friend was right here.

Doc then shared with Noel many of the stories of Billy's life and told him about spreading his ashes outside the pub. Noel said he could come up with a better place for the ashes – the grandfather clock. They signed a note about placing them in the clock. It was 1 April. Noel said: 'Let's date it 2 April because others might think it was an April fool's joke.' Then an Irish wake broke out. Doc had to be carried back to his room by some of the customers after the wake.[28]

The grandfather clock is situated very close to the picture of President John F. Kennedy in Mulligan's. Mike Carr has also supplied a first-hand account of meeting President Kennedy the day before he was assassinated:

In November 1963, President John F. Kennedy was in Texas, trying to reunite the Democratic party which had splintered between the liberals headed by Senator Ralph Yarborough and the conservatives led by Governor John Connolly. On November 21st, President Kennedy was attending a reception at the historic Rice Hotel in downtown Houston. My parents, both grassroots Democrats, had worked in President Kennedy's campaign in 1960, as had myself and my brothers, Billy and David, as workers in the Kids for Kennedy organisation. Having received an invitation to the reception, my mom and dad took all three of us with them. I remember a crowded room but all I could see was President Kennedy. His presence filled the room. My mother, Billie Carr, was standing with the President, her hand on his shoulder, asking him not to go to Dallas. She said, 'They're all crazy there.' President Kennedy patted my mom on the shoulder, saying, 'That's all right, Billie, everything will be fine.' Then, my mother called us over and introduced us to President Kennedy. She told the President that my birthday was the next day, November 22nd. The President said, 'Let me be the first to wish you a Happy Birthday.' He asked me, 'Do you know who else has a birthday tomorrow?' I said, 'Yes, John Nance Garner.' John Nance Garner, aka Cactus Jack, was the 32nd Vice-President of the United States. President Kennedy told me that he would call him tomorrow and wish him a happy birthday because he would not be able to join the motorcade. He then asked me how old I would be. I nervously said that I was going to be thirteen years old. President Kennedy said, 'Thirteen is an age when you might think you know it all, but listen and respect your mother and father, even *I* call them to ask for their advice.' Mom then introduced my brothers, David and Billy, and President Kennedy asked each of us who we liked best in the upcoming football game between University of Texas and Texas A&M. I said that I liked both teams. President Kennedy turned to my mother and said, 'Oh, he's the politician.' David said, 'I like Rice University.' President Kennedy replied, 'David is the diplomat'. Billy said, 'I don't like either one of them', to which President Kennedy said, 'And Billy must be the critic.' Then President Kennedy said it was good to meet all of us and turned to greet others.[29]

Mulligan's lost another of it loyal customers in 2012 – Con Houlihan, who died after a long illness in August of that year. Peter Roche, who had visited him many times in hospital, recalled that, on one visit, Houlihan had said to him that the doctors had ordered no visitors. Roche said he knew this was not the case, and that Houlihan was feeling too unwell to see him, but because of his innate courtesy he had softened the rejection by citing the medical staff for the restriction.[30]

Following the closure of *The Irish Press*, Houlihan famously described Mulligan's as the one bright spot in a grey world 'down there'. Had he lived, he might accept that there are now two bright spots, the other being the Vintage Kitchen restaurant beside Mulligan's, which has received glowing reviews, most notably from Paulo Tullio in the *Irish Independent*, who opened his column with a personal observation: 'It doesn't happen very often, maybe a couple of times a year, that I get really excited about a new restaurant. But it happened to me this week when I went to review the Vintage Kitchen.'[31]

Mulligan's continues to attract the attention of television producers. Two television series, *Ripper Street* and *Quirke*, used the pub to shoot interior scenes in 2013.[32] *Ripper Street* is set in Whitechapel in the East End of London in 1889, six months after the murders by Jack the Ripper. Mark Geraghty won a BAFTA Award for Television Craft: Production Design in 2014 for his work on the series. Some of the crew celebrated the win in Mulligan's in May that year, when Christy Hynes and Ger Cusack posed for photographs holding the award.[33]

Why Mulligan's has managed to remain in business when so many other greater enterprises in the vicinity have fallen is not clear. Con Houlihan may have supplied part of the answer when he wrote: 'Mulligan's is, quite simply, a great pub.'[34] It has inspired great writers and great literature. Journalists in Ireland and around the world use it as an unscientific barometer for economic policy, international sporting events and upheavals in society. The man on the Clapham omnibus in London equates to the drinker in Mulligan's.

The pub has become an inhabited museum and a fearsome 'Speakers' Corner', firmly anchored in the landscape of Dublin city. The grandfather clock in the bar is never in agreement with the wall clock in the front lounge, a discord generally reflected in the conversations of Mulligan's regulars. Despite this, laughter chimes almost as regular as the clock. There are so many facets to this institution that it defies an overarching description. Its rainbow has more than seven shades.

However, the story of Billy Brooks Carr from Texas throws more than a little light on the personality of Mulligan's. His ashes in the grandfather clock indicate that thousands of miles are no barrier to what his family consider a cherished place. Every year, his relatives and friends visit and remember him. They have made Mulligan's, in part, into a *de facto* cemetery, but one where joy and dignity sit snugly together. This much-loved man from the other side of the world has become closer than any other to the grand old pub of Poolbeg Street. Billy enjoyed visiting many sites in Dublin but his brothers had in mind a specific last resting place for him in the city. For them, there was no competition.

Only in Mulligan's.

APPENDIX A

MAP AND DESCRIPTIONS OF THE VICINITY OF MULLIGAN'S

Mulligan's is perched in an area which, in former times, had similarities to Soho in London. Indeed, the pub itself, and its well-known connection with the journalist Con Houlihan, was not unlike the relationship between the Coach and Horses, Greek Street, and the columnist Jeffrey Bernard. (His writings about adventures on the premises formed the basis of a successful play, *Jeffrey Bernard is Unwell*, by Keith Waterhouse.)

Like other bohemians in Soho, Bernard frequented many pubs in the West End, most famously The French House and The Colony Room (now closed) on Dean Street. The neighbourhood of Mulligan's is dotted with public houses, each very different in appearance and character: Bowe's, Chaplin's, the Dark Horse Inn, Doyle's, Kennedy's, The Long Stone, MacTurcaill's (which changed ownership in 2015) and O'Reilly's. The Scotch House and The Silver Swan are no more. The White Horse has been replaced by a modern building housing the Dark Horse Inn.

Hawkins Street was unusual in having a monument at both ends. John Mulligan was assaulted outside his pub in 1865 because of critical comments he was reputed to have

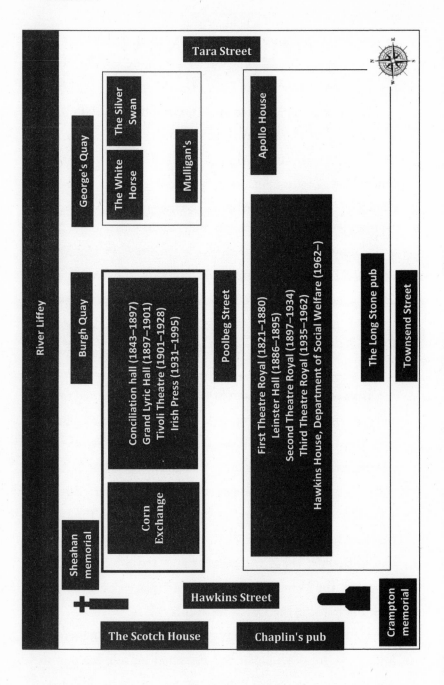

made about the Crampton monument, situated at one end of Hawkins Street. John's son, James, contributed to a fund for the Sheahan memorial, erected at the other end of Hawkins Street in memory of Constable Patrick Sheahan, who died while attempting to save workmen from a sewer in 1905.

Over the centuries, Mulligan's benefited from custom generated by large establishments such as the Corn Exchange, Conciliation Hall, which was used as a meeting place by Daniel O'Connell, five theatres and the Irish Press group of newspapers.

APPENDIX B

MAP AND DESCRIPTIONS OF MULLIGAN'S BACK BAR

1 Cast-iron fire surround and mirror.

2 Mulligan's back room. This area is known as the Joyce Room, the tabernacle, the Jockeys' Room, the parlour and the room at the back. It was the setting for one of the scenes in the short story 'Counterparts', included in James Joyce's book, *Dubliners* (1914). The description of the room and the clientèle by Joyce show that he was familiar with the pub. The room was also the setting for a scene in James Plunkett's novel *Strumpet City* (1969). In recent times it has been used as a location for the BBC Victorian crime series, *Ripper Street*, and in other television productions. Customers used to decide on horseracing bets here, which gave rise to its designation as the Jockeys' Room.

3 The grandfather clock. Irish republicans are reputed to have hidden rifles in the base of the clock during the War of Independence before Mulligan's was raided by the Black and Tans. In recent times, the ashes of a US tourist, Billy Brooks Carr, were deposited in the base of the frame. His family and friends make regular visits to Mulligan's from Billy's native Texas to celebrate his life and memory.

4 Photograph of President John F. Kennedy. This photograph marks the visit of Kennedy to Mulligan's in 1947. He was accompanied by a journalist with *The Irish Press*, Jack Grealish,

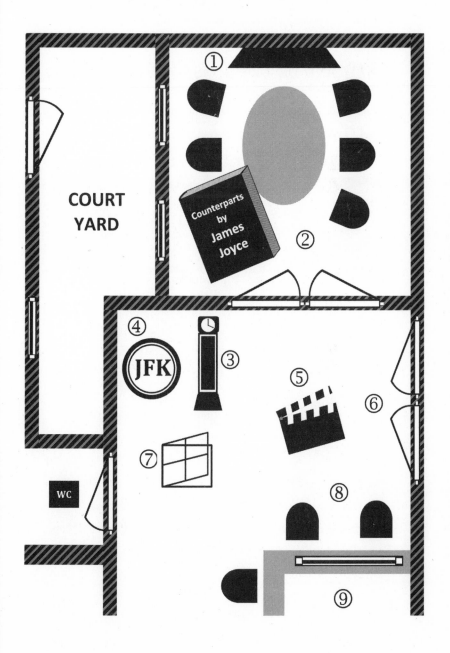

who had to borrow money from one of his colleagues to buy the future US president a drink. Kennedy was a fan of Joyce, and recognised the pub as the one mentioned in Joyce's short story 'Counterparts'.

5   This bar has been popular as a location for films and television productions. The BBC television drama *Quirke*, starring Michael Gambon and Gabriel Byrne, was filmed here. It was also used for scenes in the Irish crime film *Dead Bodies*.

6   Entrance to the back lounge.

7   Skylight.

8   Nuts' Corner. This area, at the far end of the counter, was once a favoured spot for several regulars to meet and converse. They named the area Nuts' Corner, a designation it has kept to this day.

9   Serving area. The interior of this area and the front bar is characterised by Victorian mahogany panelling. Privacy dividers are positioned at either end of the counter.

APPENDIX C

MAP AND DESCRIPTIONS OF MULLIGAN'S
FRONT BAR

1   Alcove.

2   Original Victorian-style gas lamps above the counter.

3   Entrances to the front lounge.

4   Large wine cask, sectioned and used as a privacy divider.

5   Cellar hatch.

6   Supporting beam on which is painted 'John Mulligan'.

7   Supporting beam on which is painted 'Est. 1782'.

8   Hallway and stairs.

9   Entrance doors from Poolbeg Street. A horseshoe is fixed into the ceiling area of the entrance doors. This may have been placed there for good luck. John Mulligan's son, James, was a keen pony-trotter. Near the entrance doors, rings are bolted into the ceiling. These are reputed to have been used for hanging a weighing scales and vegetable and fruit baskets when the premises operated as a spirit grocery. A set replicating this area of the premises was used for scenes in the Oscar-winning film, *My Left Foot*.

10 Peter Roche was described by the journalist, Con Houlihan, as Mulligan's unofficial public relations officer. He is known as P.R. and as 'Dr Roche'. The area where he sits has become known as Roche's corner. Tourists and historians who visit Mulligan's are welcomed by 'Dr Roche' and made to feel at home.

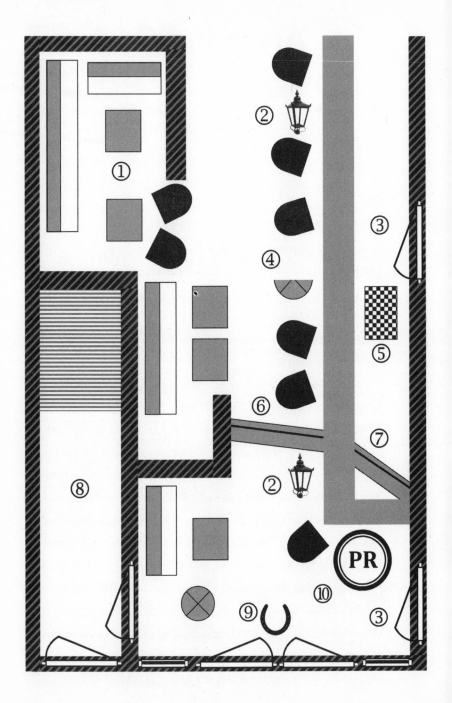

APPENDIX D

MAP AND DESCRIPTIONS OF MULLIGAN'S BACK LOUNGE

1 Former entrances to WCs on either side. These were blocked off in the early 1970s. In late 2014 a new ladies WC, a beer garden and a smoking area were constructed.

2 Victorian mirrors.

3 Five engravings of Shakespeare plays, a legacy of the time when Mulligan's was a theatre bar catering for the performers and patrons of nearby theatres, including three named the Theatre Royal, the first of which was built in 1821 and the last of which closed down in 1962.

All the engravings were published by J. & J. Boydell. The Boydell Shakespeare folio included 167 engravings, dating from 1791 to 1803, which were adapted from paintings shown at the Shakespeare Gallery in London in the late eighteenth century. John Boydell (1719–1804) was a noted engraver, publisher, print-seller, and even lord mayor of London, who established the Shakespeare Gallery and sold engravings of the paintings to subscribers. His nephew, Josiah Boydell, published the collected engravings after John Boydell's death.

The year of publication is given in each of the descriptions following, but the engravings may be copies from a later era:

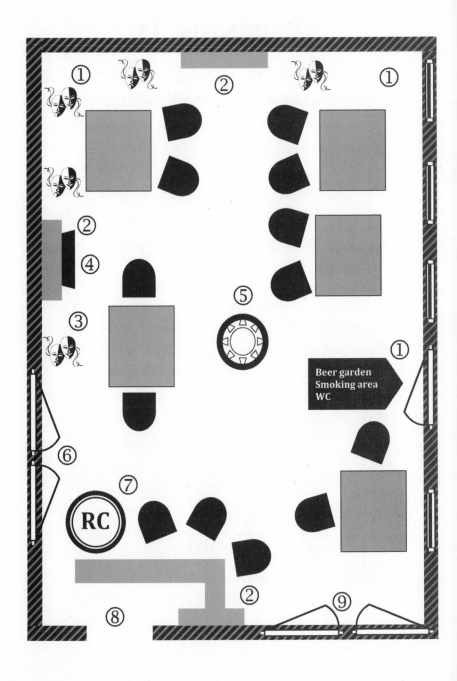

All's Well That Ends Well, Act V, Scene III (1796) as engraved by G. S. and J. G. Facius, after the painting by Francis Wheatley.

Two Gentlemen of Verona, Act V, Scene III (1792) as engraved by Luigi Schiavonetti (1765–1810). The engraving depicts a forest scene with Valentine, Proteus, Silvia and Julia. (The scene depicted in this engraving originates not from Act V, Scene III, as stated, but from Act V, Scene IV.)

A Comedy of Errors, Act V, Scene I (1800) as engraved by C. G. Playter, after the painting by I. F. Rigaud.

King Henry IV, Part I, Act II, Scene IV (1796) as engraved by R. Thew.

Love's Labour's Lost, Act IV, Scene I (1793) as engraved by Thomas Ryder.

4 Fireplace.
5 Carved mahogany ceiling rose.
6 Entrance to the back bar.
7 RC: this area is known as Rambo's corner, called after Robert Sweeney, one of Mulligan's most loyal customers. Tourists are often invited to have pictures taken with him.
8 Entrance to the front lounge serving area.
9 Entrance to the front lounge.

APPENDIX E

MAP AND DESCRIPTIONS OF MULLIGAN'S FRONT LOUNGE

1 Eight playbills on silk behind a glass casing. These relate to productions at the second Theatre Royal (Hippodrome):

> *The Colleen Bawn*, 'for the benefit of families of Irish soldiers killed in South Africa', 14 December 1899.
>
> *Cyrano de Bergerac*, with Charles Wyndham, founder of Wyndham's Theatre, London, in the lead role, 12 March 1900, described as 'a state performance by command of their excellencies, the Lord Lieutenant K.G. [George Cadogan, 5th Earl Cadogan] and Lady Cadogan'.
>
> *The Idler*, with George Alexander in the lead role of Martin Cross, 20 November 1901.
>
> *Richard II*, with Herbert Beerbohm Tree, founder of the Royal Academy of Dramatic Art, in the lead role, 26 April 1904.
>
> *Faust*, 3 May 1906.
>
> *The Only Way*, starring Martin Harvey, 24 November 1906.
>
> *The Corsican Brothers,* starring Martin Harvey, 5 November 1906.
>
> *Peter Pan*, 4 April 1907.

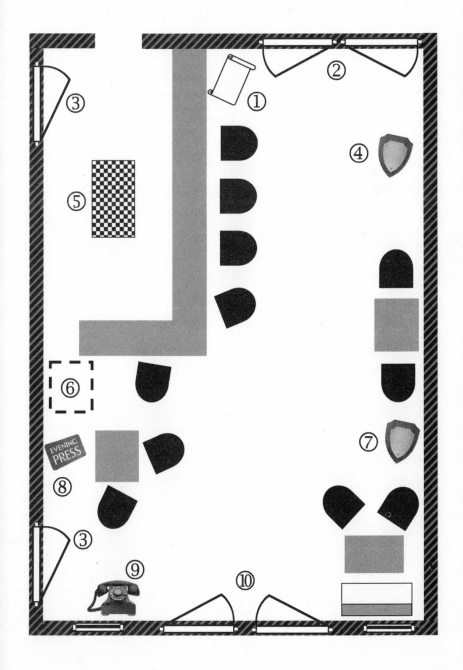

2   Entrance to the back lounge.

3   Entrances to the front bar.

4   Plaque commemorating the author and journalist, Con Houli-han.

5   Cellar hatch in the serving area. On the wall behind the serving area hangs a signed card by Eusebio, a picture of Mick Byrne (Butterkrust) and another of Christy Murphy, who was known as Barber. This last photograph, taken in the 1950s by Colman Doyle, catches Murphy grinning, resting his chin on his fist. In *Ireland – 40 years of Photo-journalism*, by Doyle and Liam Flynn, the caption to the reproduced photograph describes Murphy as a docker who lived in Luke Street near Mulligan's. The caption adds: 'Under the picture is the legend "Computers how are ye", a phrase he uttered to the drinking concourse when he was informed that soon everything would be worked by computer. He did not live to see the reality.'

6   Area where Mulligan's phone booth used to stand.

7   Joyce plaque.

8   Copy of the *Evening Press* signed by some of its journalists.

9   Mulligan's public telephone.

10 Entrance from Poolbeg Street.

ENDNOTES

Abbreviations

CFP	Cusack family papers
DDA	Dublin Diocesan Archives
DIT	Dublin Institute of Technology
EH	*Evening Herald*
EP	*Evening Press*
FJ	*The Freeman's Journal*
IFHF	Irish Family History Foundation
IE	*Irish Examiner*
II	*Irish Independent*
IP	*The Irish Press*
IT	*The Irish Times*
NAI	National Archives of Ireland
NLI	National Library of Ireland
NUJ	National Union of Journalists
NMSA	National Monuments Service Archive, Dublin
ROD	Registry of Deeds, Henrietta Street, Dublin
SI	*Sunday Independent*

1   Counter Hatched

1   Colm Lennon, *Irish Historic Towns Atlas, No. 19: Dublin, Part II, 1610 to 1756* (2008), p. 6. One of the earliest mentions of Poolbeg Street can be found in a deed involving William Alcock, Dublin, gentleman, and Nathanial Dyer, Dublin,

shipwright, dated 26 March 1715, which referred to 'a new street called or intended to be called Polebegg Street', ROD, Alcock to Dyer 14–305–6275.

2 Sir John Rogerson (1648–1724) was lord mayor of Dublin (1693–4) and an MP (Clogher 1692–3, Dublin city 1695–1703). A quay located close to Poolbeg Street is named after him.

3 His surname suggests Dutch or German ancestry. Schults and its variants, however, are not to be found among records of the Dutch Huguenots who sought sanctuary in Dublin because of persecution in their homeland.

4 ROD, Crowther to Schults 62–400–43385; Murphy to Schults 167–202–111976; Schults to Fleming 212–188–138891; Schults to Fleming 291–554–192853; Fleming to Schults 388–234–257814; Schults to King 62–401–43386; Schults to King 79–280–55827; Taylor to Schults 158–408–101984; Jackson to Schults 175–320–117220; Barclay to Schults 181–580–121823; Schults to Nowland 198–512–133384; Schults to Cane 257–125–165790; Schults to Lilly 380–680–258345; Schults to King 388–444–258614. The trade of block-maker may be applied to the making of blocks for buildings or to the shaping of chunks of wood used in ship-building.

5 ROD, Murphy to Schults 167–202–111976.

6 The buildings which Mulligan's of Poolbeg Street occupies at present are Nos 8 (bar) and 9 (lounge bar and back lounge). The sign above the premises extends over No. 10. These street numbers have changed over the years. Nos 8 and 9 were 17 and 18 up to 1835; from 1836 to 1844 they became 13 and 14; and

from 1845 to the present day they have been Nos 8 and 9. The descriptions in this text use the present-day street numbering system, with the street numbers at the time given here in parentheses. The first grocer recorded at the address of 8 (17) Poolbeg Street is Henry Murphy, who occupied the premises from at least 1761 to 1774 (*Wilson's Dublin Directories*). The street directory listings began in a haphazard way and for many years updating and correction was very slow. No street number is given in the directories before 1775, but a deed (ROD, Schults to Fleming 212–188–138891) cites Henry Murphy in 1760 as being in a building that can be identified as No. 8 (17) Poolbeg Street. A Henry Murphy operated as a grocer in Poolbeg Street in the mid-1700s but there is no evidence to link the two Henrys. There is no listing for 8 (17) or 9 (18) Poolbeg Street in the directories for 1775–83. Moses Walsh is listed as being a grocer at 9 (18) Poolbeg Street in 1784–5. The next listing that appears is 1787 for Talbot Fyan. He is described as a grocer and the address is given as No. 9 (18). The grocery moved next door to No. 8 (17) in 1794, where Fyan remained for fifty years, retiring in 1844. While there is no occupier listed for 1782, the year cited as the start of the business, the evidence to suggest that Walsh and/or his relative Fyan began trading that year is strong. Birth records show that both families were in the area long before 1782. The fact that 1782 has been displayed on the premises, inside and above the entrance door to No. 8, and in all subsequent records, lends weight to that date being the year of the birth of the business.

7   NLI, DU–RC–BA–147626.

8   *Wilson's Dublin Directory*, 1787.

9   Talbot Fyan's wife, Mary, and Moses Walsh are likely to have been blood relatives. According to the birth certificate of one of the Fyans' children, Talbert [*sic*], in 1808, Mary's maiden name is given as Walsh (NLI, DU–RC–BA–349857). Moses Walsh and his wife, Catherine, are recorded as having two children: Edward in 1777 (NLI, DU–RC–BA–595187) and Moses in 1787 (NLI, DU–RC–BA–153021). When Moses Walsh (born 1787) married in 1817, Mary Fyan stood as a witness (NLI, DU–RC–MA–28423).

10   Shops that sold fruit, vegetables and spirits became known as spirit grocers. However, some also sold hardware items and sundry goods. In legal terms, a spirit grocer was described as 'any person dealing in or selling tea, cocoa-nuts, chocolate or pepper, and having an excise licence to sell spirits by retail in any quantity not exceeding two quarts at any one time to be consumed elsewhere than on the premises where sold', *Journals of the House of Lords*, Vol. CIV (1872), p. 737.

11   Nicholas N. Donnelly, *History of Dublin Parishes*, Vol. II (1910), p. 159.

12   During Talbot Fyan's lifetime, Poolbeg Street stretched from Hawkins Street to Moss Street. With the building of Tara Street railway station in the late nineteenth century, part of the street was cut away and it now extends from Hawkins Street to Luke Street.

13   *Wilson's Dublin Directories*. Entries for Poolbeg Street: Jeremiah Shaw, biscuit maker, 1784 and 1786.

14   No. 8 Poolbeg Street, now Mulligan's bar, still includes features distinctive to Dutch Billys even though the structure has been

modified greatly over the years. This architectural design began to fall from grace in Dublin in the mid- to late eighteenth century. 'Dutch Billys were reputedly named after William of Orange. Their arrival in Dublin is generally attributed to an influx of French Huguenots after 1685 and to Dutch and Flemish Protestants fleeing persecution after 1690', Maurice Craig, *Dublin 1660–1860: The Shaping of the City* (1980), pp. 86–87.

15 Dr Robin Usher, *Protestant Dublin, 1660–1760: Architecture and Iconography* (2012), p. 95.

16 The church was built in the early 1720s and fell into disuse in the mid-nineteenth century. An excavation of the site in 1992 includes a report on skeletal remains of at least twelve individuals (eleven adult, one juvenile) from what is believed to have been the church graveyard. One skull showed signs that the deceased had once been such an ardent pipe smoker that he had, over the years, successively ground down his teeth. NMSA 92E0098, Channing, John, 'Report on Archaeological Monitoring and Excavations at Poolbeg, Dublin 2' (1992); Buckley, Laureen, 'Tara Street/Poolbeg Street Skeletal Report' (1992).

17 Steven C. Smyrl, *Dictionary of Dublin Dissent – Dublin's Protestant Dissenting Meeting Houses, 1660–1920* (2009), pp. 178–195. Schulze (*c.* 1763–1839) was minister at the Dutch church in Poolbeg Street from 1806 to 1839.

18 Henry F. Berry, *A History of the Royal Dublin Society* (1915), p. 97. The Dublin Society became the Royal Dublin Society in 1820. The society had buildings on both sides of Poolbeg Street. These housed a laboratory, a repository for agricultural implements, fossils and minerals.

19 *Wilson's Dublin Directories* – Thomas Hicks was listed as a Poolbeg Street resident, 1784–90; Robert Hall was listed as a Poolbeg Street resident, 1790–5.

20 Irish Architectural Archive: http://www.iarc.ie (accessed 26 June 2013).

21 Walter G. Strickland, *A Dictionary of Irish Artists*, Vol. II (1913), pp. 100–102.

22 Mairéad Reynolds, 'James Donovan, Dublin china merchants', *Irish Arts Review*, Vol. 2, No. 3 (1985), p. 28.

23 *Wilson's Dublin Directories* – Traynor is spelled as Trennor and Trinner. He is recorded as living in Poolbeg Street from 1791–94.

24 Thomas Davis, *The Speeches of the Rt. Hon. John Philpot Curran* (1868), pp. 196–205. The trial was held on 25 June 1794. Dr Drennan was defended by the celebrated orator and politician, John Philpot Curran. Traynor was also mentioned in the case of William Michael Byrne for high treason in 1798. Evidence was given that Thomas Traynor of Poolbeg Street had been at a seditious meeting but had escaped. See Thomas Jones Howell, *A Complete Collection of State Trials and Proceedings for High Treason*, Vol. XXVII (1820), p. 463.

25 ROD, Tandy to Tandy 473–257–300.

26 William Cobbett, *Cobbett's Annual Register*, July to September 1802, Vol. II (1803), pp. 648–649; 'Napper Tandy had been apprehended, tried, convicted and condemned: France snatched him from justice, with the halter about his neck, and compelled us to convey him, in one of our own ships, in triumph to her coast. There, my lord, in that act, I greatly

fear, that loyalty, public spirit, and national character, in this country, received a blow from which they will never recover.'

27 *FJ*, 16 November 1776.

28 *Ibid.*, 5 March 1808.

29 Rev. James Whitelaw, *An Essay on the Population of Dublin* (1805), p. 113.

30 *FJ*, 8 June 1799; Frank Hopkins, *Hidden Dublin: Deadbeats, Dossers and Decent Skins* (2007), p. 72.

31 *FJ*, 29 November 1806, 25 November 1807, 22 November 1808.

32 *Ibid.*, 4 September 1809; 23 November 1825.

33 *Ibid.*, 23 November 1825; 18 November 1836.

34 Rev. G. N. Wright, *An Historical Guide to Ancient and Modern Dublin* (1821), p. 322.

35 *FJ*, 19 January 1821.

36 *Ibid.*, 23 August 1821.

37 *Ibid.*, 21 September 1818. The householders in the parish expressed their outrage that a minister of the crown should have the 'discretionary power of admitting light and air into the habitations of the sick, first exciting fever in all its frightful varieties, through the necessities of the people shutting up their windows and hearths and then with extorted compassion, taunting the last agonies of his victims by a proclamation for the free ventilation of their bodies, ere the coffin entombs them'.

38 *Ibid.*, 14 February 1825.

39 *Ibid.*, 24 April 1829.

40   *Ibid.*, 12 June 1835.

41   *Ibid.*, 24 August 1836.

42   *Ibid.*, 1 April 1843.

43   Thomas Francis Meagher delivered his 'Sword speech' in the building in 1846, which led to the Young Irelanders seceding from the Repeal movement.

44   Glasnevin Trust. Mary Fyan died on 5 May 1842.

45   *FJ*, 17, 19, 22 June 1846.

46   Glasnevin Trust. Fyan died on 9 April 1851.

47   NAI, Landed Estate Court Files, 069–50–1858.

2   Counter Attack

1   ROD, Halpin to Mulligan 10–114–244; *Wilson's Dublin Directories* – entries for 8 Poolbeg Street: Alicia Halpin, grocer, 1847–52; Thomas Halpin, grocer and spirit dealer, Townsend Street, 1836–71. The family connection, if any, between Thomas Halpin and Alicia Halpin is not clear.

2   NLI, DU–RC–MA–71480, Marriage of John Mulligan to Alicia Halpin. IFHF, birth of John Mulligan 11 July 1825 to James Mulligan and Marcella Keegan at Moynalvey, County Meath. *Wilson's Dublin Directories* – entries for Poolbeg Street: John Mulligan, grocer and spirit dealer, 1853–75. The same John Mulligan is also listed as running a grocery at 29 Nicholas Street, Dublin, 1859–76. Mulligan died in 1875 but the directory listings were not updated for 1876. It was common for such listings not to be updated.

3   The children born to James and Marcella Mulligan were: Thomas (1816), Anne (1817), Bridget (1819), Mary (1821),

Patrick (1823), John (1825), Philip (1828), James (1833) and Thomas (1838). It is likely that their first-born child, Thomas, died, as their last child was also given this name.

4   *FJ*, 3 December 1852.

5   *Ibid.*, 10 December 1852.

6   *Ibid.*, 10 January 1854; 8 October 1860. Mulligan contributed money to the Dargan Institute, to be used to establish an art gallery, and to another fund set up to support the families of two men who had died in a scaffolding accident in Portobello Gardens, Dublin.

7   *Ibid.*, 4 November 1865.

8   The connection between Joyce and Mulligan's was publicised on the façade of the pub in 1974, when the artist and signwriter, James Cassidy, carried out considerable restoration work. He used the front of No. 10 as a large canvas on which he painted an elegant Mulligan's overhead sign and a decorative roll commemorating Bloomsday, with the insignia: *Do chum Glóire Dé agus Onóra na hÉireann* (To the Glory of God and the Honour of Ireland). The phrase was also the motto of the Pioneer Total Abstinence Association and appeared for many years on the masthead of *The Irish Press*, which copied it from the dedication at the beginning of the *Annals of the Four Masters* (O'Donovan, 1854). Richard Levins and his staff applied their artistic hands to the façades of Nos 8, 9 and 10 in the summer of 2014.

9   The pantomime was *Ali Baba and the Forty Thieves*.

10 *FJ*, 14 January 1868.

11 *IT*, 24 January 1868; *FJ*, 24 January 1868.

12 *IT*, 14 April 1868; *FJ*, 18 April 1868.

13 CFP. The contract, dated 12 March 1874, is made between John Mulligan and George Booker, house painter, 162 Great Britain Street (now Parnell Street), Dublin, and headed 'Estimate for painting and papering to be done to new house in Poolbeg St for Mr John Mulligan'.

14 Glasnevin Trust. John Mulligan died on 9 February 1875.

15 NAI, 'Wills and Administrations (extracts) 1875'.

3 Counter Intelligence

1 Dublin street directories cite John Mulligan as having a spirit grocer's at 29 Nicholas Street from 1853 to 1876. His address, which was recorded in Glasnevin Cemetery at the time of his death, is given as 8 Poolbeg Street and Torca View, Dalkey, County Dublin. James Mulligan's address at the time of his marriage was 2 Westbury Road, Rathgar, Dublin. The birth certificate for James's daughter, Mary Alicia, gives both his and her place of birth as 78 Eccles Street, Dublin. This house is known as Bloom House because it is believed to be the same design as No. 7, which fell into disrepair and was eventually knocked down to make way for an extension to the Mater Misericordiae hospital. James Joyce's close friend, J. F. Byrne, lived at 7 Eccles Street. The author used the address for Bloom's residence.

2 CFP. Anastasia and James Mulligan contracted George Booker, 162 Great Britain Street (now Parnell Street), Dublin, to carry out some improvements. The contract is dated 22 May 1876, Dublin. The body of the contract reads:

'I propose to prepare and paint with four coats best lead and oil paint the new large room and walls and ceilings off shop and small room off shop finished; walls French green, ceilings white and cornices ornamented and with gilt moulding, wash and clean all the oak painting and ceiling and varnish same inside of shop.

'Prepare and paint the outside of windows on fronts of old and new houses and cement work two coats and four coats on new cement work of stores, pillasters [*sic*] grained green marble gates and doors painted and grained oak and varnished also inside of doors in stores grained oak.

'Funding all materials for above work of the best description and finish same in a proper manner for the sum of forty seven pounds sterling.' [Underneath the words 'forty seven pounds', which have been struck through, is written 'forty five pounds'.]

3   *FJ*, 15 December 1876.

4   *IT*, 26 August 1882.

5   *Ibid.*, 22 October 1883.

6   *FJ*, 5 September 1883.

7   *IT*, 31 July 1886.

8   *Ibid.*, 27 June 1888.

9   *Ibid.*, 13 July 1889.

10 CFP, Paddy Flynn, in an interview with Kathleen O'Connor, 1983, courtesy of George Pujolas.

11 The Hibernian Bank was founded in 1825 and was taken over by the Bank of Ireland in 1958. The shares held by James and their value (at the time) were listed in his will (1931): Hibernian Bank, £19,000; Boland's Limited, £35; Dublin

Distillers, £12 and the Dublin Theatre Company, which ran the Theatre Royal (1897–1934), £2,460.

12 *FJ*, 23 February 1878; 4 May 1887; 3 June 1905. Among the institutions and causes to which James Mulligan gave donations were the Augustinian Fathers, for the building of a presbytery in John Street, Dublin (1878); the Christian Brothers School, St Andrew's, Westland Row, Dublin (1887); and the family of Constable John Sheahan after his death while attempting to save people from a sewer in Burgh Quay, Dublin (1905).

13 *II*, 28 January 1919; *IT*, 9 March 1931.

14 *IT*, 9 March 1931.

15 NAI, James Mulligan's will (1931).

16 *IT*, 11 February 1880.

17 *FJ*, 3 November 1886.

18 *Ibid.*, 6 February 1893.

19 *Ibid.*, 14 December 1897.

20 *IT*, 27 November 1897; 25 October 1901. The Grand Lyric Theatre (1897) became known as the Lyric Theatre of Varieties the following year, and was renamed again in October 1901 as the Tivoli Variety Theatre.

21 *FJ*, 2 May 1891.

22 NAI, 1901 census. Apart from the six workers who lived at No. 8 Poolbeg Street, the other residents were James and Anastasia Mulligan, their daughter Mary, James's brother-in-law John Gray, and James's cousin Anastasia Doran.

23 Jan Kelly, in a written communication to the author, 2014.

24 *IT*, 9 March 1931. Sir Henry Irving (1838–1905), Herbert

Beerbohm Tree (1852–1917), Fred Terry (1863–1933), Julia Neilson (1858–1967), Ellen Terry (1847–1928) and Sir J. Forbes-Robertson (1853–1937) were the leading English stage actors of their time.

25 Seán O'Donohoe, in an interview with the author, 2014.

26 *II*, 9 March 1931.

27 At the time of the Lock-out, some 20,000 workers were fighting for the right to unionise against around 300 employers, chief among those being William Martin Murphy, chairman of the Dublin United Tramway Company.

28 *FJ*, 11 June 1891.

29 *IT*, 20 December 1913.

30 Richard Ellmann, *James Joyce* (1982), p. 208.

31 From the short story 'Counterparts', published in James Joyce, *Dubliners* (London), pp. 81–82. Smahan means a small amount of whiskey.

32 Letter to Stanislaus Joyce, 23 August 1912, quoted in Richard Ellmann, *James Joyce* (1982), pp. 331–332.

33 Postcard to Stanislaus Joyce, *c.* 26 August 1912, quoted in *Letters of James Joyce*, Vol. II (1966) edited by Richard Ellmann, p. 314.

34 CFP, Paddy Flynn, in an interview with Kathleen O'Connor, 1983, courtesy of George Pujolas.

35 *FJ* and *IT*, 14 February 1921.

36 Ger Cusack, in an interview with the author, 2014.

37 Glasnevin Trust. Anastasia Mulligan died on 29 April 1921. Two months after her death, on 6 June 1921, James paid £12

6s to Glasnevin Marble Works, Farrell & Son, for the firm to thoroughly renovate the family grave, where Anastasia had been interred (CFP).

38 The solicitor George Drevar Fottrell (1814–87) had been retained by James's father, John, since at least 1855. Fottrell graduated from the King's Inns law school in Dublin in 1831, having been admitted when he was thirteen. His office was based at 57 Lower Dominick Street, Dublin, until the 1860s, when he moved to 46 Fleet Street, Dublin. He died on 7 January 1887 after being run down by a drunken carriage driver in O'Connell Street. His son, George Drevar Fottrell, Jnr (1849–1925), took over the family business, which continued to be retained by James Mulligan. Fottrell Jnr was appointed clerk of the crown and peace for County Dublin in 1888, an office he occupied until his retirement in 1919, when he was made a Knight Commander of the Order of the Bath. The lengthy business association James enjoyed with Fottrell Jnr lasted more than three decades. Fottrell Jnr was cited twice in Joyce's *Ulysses*: in the Cyclops episode (p. 447) and in the Circe episode (p. 587) (James Joyce, *Ulysses*, Penguin edition, 1992).

39 ROD, 1928–16–28.

40 *II*, 17 December 1927. The marriage certificate of O'Brien and Mary Alicia Mulligan could not be found. They were married between 1901 (where she is described in the census of that year as single) and 1911 (when she is designated as married). O'Brien, a solicitor, was the second surviving son of Prof. S. P. O'Brien of Waterford, and was a brother of Rev. D. O'Brien of Auckland, New Zealand, of Mr S. O'Brien, BL, of London, of Mr A. P. O'Brien of Waterford, and of Mrs W. P. English of

Newry. He was admitted as a solicitor in 1906. In his younger days, O'Brien was a prominent member of Waterford Boat Club and a successful competitor on the cycle-racing tracks. He was a member of the Howth Yachting Club. During the First World War, he volunteered and saw active service in France with the rank of staff sergeant major. His wife, Mary Alicia, died on 22 December 1945.

41 NAI, James Mulligan's will (1931). Dr Lennon began seeing James in 1927. His fees up to James's death amounted to more than £500.

42 CFP, Paddy Flynn, in an interview with Kathleen O'Connor, 1983, courtesy of George Pujolas.

43 *IT*, 9 March 1931. The obituary notice for James Mulligan incorrectly put his age at seventy-eight years.

44 *II*, 9 March 1931.

45 *IT*, 9 March 1931.

4   Press Thunders, Stage Lights

1 Michael Smith already owned property in the vicinity. He had bought 7a Poolbeg Street from Edward Dwyer in 1929.

2 NAI. The 1901 census lists a Michael Smith, grocer's assistant from County Cavan, living at 40 Watling Street, Dublin. Con Cusack recalled that Michael Smith, his uncle, worked for a time in a pub in Parnell Street, Dublin, before he was employed at Mulligan's. The 1911 census situates him in Mulligan's, along with seven other residents: James and Anastasia Mulligan, and assistants Michael Ryan (29), a native of Tipperary; Edward Kealy (25), Wexford; James McGrath (17), Mayo; Patrick Fry

(29), Meath, described as a porter; and Ellen Williams (54), Wexford, a general domestic servant.

3   CFP, Paddy Flynn, in an interview with Kathleen O'Connor, 1983, courtesy of George Pujolas.

4   Kevin C. Kearns, *Dublin Pub Life and Lore – An Oral History* (1997), p. 37.

5   DDA, AB8/B/XV/a. Following a strong campaign by the Irish National Teachers' Organisation these codes were amended. At a general meeting of the Catholic hierarchy in Maynooth in 1942, the prelates raised no objection to modification of the code barring women teachers from marrying publicans.

6   Cork 1–6, Kilkenny 1–6 (6 September 1931); first replay Cork 2–5, Kilkenny 2–5 (11 October 1931); second replay Cork 5–8, Kilkenny 3–4 (1 November 1931).

7   *IP,* 8 September 1981.

8   In 1932 de Valera refused to continue to reimburse Britain with the 'land annuities'. These derived from financial loans granted by Britain to Irish tenant farmers to enable them to purchase land under the Irish Land Acts enacted during the previous half century. De Valera's stance resulted in the 'Economic War'. Both countries placed unilateral trade restrictions on each other and the damage to the Irish economy was severe.

9   Philip B. Ryan, *The Lost Theatres of Dublin* (1998), p. 43.

10   *SI,* 4 March 1934.

11   *IP,* 27 June 1934. The fact that there was seed (possibly for sale) on the premises to feed the pigeons might indicate that Mulligan's had not, by this time, moved to being a pub in the sense that it is defined today. The business may have been selling

other products at that time, a legacy of its origins as a spirit grocery. Headed Mulligan's notepaper from 1966 described the business as 'Grocers, Tea, Wine & Spirit Merchants'. However, this notepaper may have been printed years or perhaps decades earlier. There are hardly any indications to show when Mulligan's stopped selling sundry goods, but it appears to have been some time in the 1930s.

12 Cavan defeated Kildare by 3–6 to 2–5.

13 Kearns, *Dublin Pub Life and Lore,* p. 36.

14 Ryan, *The Lost Theatres of Dublin*, p. 41.

15 *II*, 13 September 1939.

16 Flann O'Brien, 'The trade in Dublin', *The Bell,* Vol. I, No. 2, November 1940.

17 Ryan, *The Lost Theatres of Dublin,* p. 55.

18 Peter Roche, in an interview with the author, 2014.

19 *IP*, 2 September 1994.

20 Mary O'Neill (née Roche), in conversation with the author, 2014. NAI, Mary O'Brien's will (1946). Queen Victoria visited Dublin 4–26 April 1900. CFP: in 1947 Michael Smith paid £70 to have the Mulligan family grave at Glasnevin cemetery dressed continually.

21 *IP*, 17 October 1990.

5 After the Rainbow, Before Camelot

1 Anthony Grealish, a son of Jack Grealish, in an interview with the author, 2014.

2 Jack Grealish (1910–77), a native of Galway city, joined the local *Connacht Tribune* as a cub reporter in the mid-1920s. He

was appointed assistant news editor of *The Irish Press* before its launch in 1931. He was later appointed news editor and it was when he held this title that John F. Kennedy called on him at the *Irish Press* offices in 1947. Shortly afterwards, Grealish moved to Limerick, where he became editor of the *Limerick Leader*. During his tenure he doubled the circulation of that publication. He returned to Dublin in 1955 and worked as the assistant editor of the *Sunday Review*. This posting allowed him, for the second time, to see the first print run of a national newspaper, as he had also been present for the printing of the initial copies of *The Irish Press*. Following the closure of the *Sunday Review* in 1963, he worked with Conor Cruise O'Brien at the Irish News Agency and filed court reports for *The Irish Times*. He was appointed a sub-editor of the *Irish Independent* in 1965, a position he held until his retirement in 1975. Grealish had a reputation for precision in the use of English, which he combined with a natural flair for writing crisp and accurate reports. He is remembered by his contemporaries as 'the news editors' news editor'.

3   *The Sign* was a US Catholic monthly publication that was published from 1921 to 1982.

4   CFP, Paddy Flynn in an interview with Kathleen O'Connor 1983, courtesy of George Pujolas.

5   Joseph Roddy, 'They cried the rain down that night', *Look*, 17 November 1964, p. 79.

6   Recollection of Anthony Grealish. In his book, *Nora Barnacle Joyce: A Portrait* (1982), p. 113, the author, Pádraic Ó Laoi, wrote: 'Kathleen [Barnacle] worked as a bookbinder in O'Gorman's and later in [*sic*] the *Connacht Tribune*'.

7   Liston was agriculture correspondent of *The Irish Press* and a founding member of the NUJ in Ireland.

8   Michael O'Toole, *More Kicks Than Pence* (1992), p. 10.

9   Kearns, *Dublin Pub Life and Lore,* p. 40.

10   Seán O'Donohoe, in an interview with the author, 2014.

11   *Ibid.*

12   *IT*, 7 April 1988.

13   Seán O'Donohoe (born 1924) is a native of Clonegal village in County Wexford. His mother was a schoolteacher and his father was an officer in the Civic Guard. After his arrival in Dublin in 1943, Seán worked in Guinan's (later O'Dwyer's) in Mount Street. Later, he worked in Gaffney's of Fairview. He played for the Banba football club, most of whose players were bar workers. This association drew him into contact with Mulligan's manager, Paddy Flynn, whose brother Ned also played for the team. When Seán was asked to work in Mulligan's in 1951 he immediately accepted Flynn's offer. He remained there until 1963, after which he was employed by Paddy Belton at the Towers pub in Ballymun. He retired in 1983.

14   Seán O'Donohoe, in an interview with the author, 2014. Andrews and Bourke were married at the Church of Corpus Christi, Griffith Avenue, Dublin, on 7 November 1951. The reception took place in the Four Provinces House, Harcourt Street.

15   Frank Gerold, *Judy* (1999), p. 341.

16   Conor Doyle, from a recollection of Christina Doyle, in conversation with the author, 2014.

17 Seán O'Donohoe, in an interview with the author, 2014. Nat King Cole performed matinee and evening shows at the Theatre Royal on 8 and 9 April 1954.

18 *Ibid.*

19 Éamonn MacThomáis, *The Labour and the Royal* (1979), p. 83.

20 Seán O'Donohoe, in an interview with the author, 2014.

21 Recollection of Micheál Smyth, in a communication to the author, 2014.

22 Scores were Cavan 2–11, Kerry 2–7 (1947); Cavan 4–5, Mayo 4–4 (1948); Cavan 2–4, Meath 1–7 (1952); Cavan 0–9, Meath 0–5 (replay, 1952).

23 Recollection of Micheál Smyth, in a communication to the author, 2014.

24 *IT*, 30 November 1956.

25 *Ibid.*, 4 April 1986.

26 O'Toole, 'Introduction', *More Kicks Than Pence*, p. ii.

27 Seán O'Donohoe, in an interview with the author, 2014.

28 *Ibid.*

29 *Ibid.* A report of the purchase of the hotel appeared in *The Kerryman*, 3 March 1961. Seán O'Donohoe was also friendly with the former RTÉ sports commentator, Mick Dunne, and the film stuntman, Jack E. Plant.

30 *Ibid.*

31 *II*, 10 June 1955.

32 Recollection of Micheál Smyth, in a communication to the author, 2014.

33 NAI, Michael Smith's will (schedule of assets), 1962.

34 CFP, Paddy Flynn, in an interview with Kathleen O'Connor, 1983, courtesy of George Pujolas.

35 Seán O'Donohoe, in an interview with the author, 2014.

36 Ger Cusack, in an interview with the author, 2014.

37 *IP*, 1 March 1957.

38 Tommy McDonald (1929–2000) was a native of Cootehill, County Cavan. At sixteen years of age he moved to England, where he worked as a barman in Luton. He returned to Ireland after a few years and worked in Brady's pub and the Viscount pub, Swords Road, Dublin, before joining Mulligan's, where he was almost immediately given the nickname Briscoe because it was said he had a likeness to the politician, Robert Briscoe. He met his wife-to-be, Eileen Brady of Killoughter, County Cavan, through their shared love of dancing. She worked for the sweetshop chain Skeffingtons. They married in 1962 and had two daughters, Evelyn and Imelda. Outside work Tommy was a dedicated family man, who spent most of the year looking forward to the two-week holiday he spent with his wife and children in August. He retired from Mulligan's in June 1993 because of ill health. His funeral in May 2000 was one of the largest in Dublin that year.

39 Recollection of Micheál Smyth, in a communication to the author, 2014.

6   Bar Change

1 NAI, Michael Smith's will, 1962. Gerard Sweetman served as Minister for Finance in Ireland from 1954 to 1957.

2 Ryan, *The Lost Theatres of Dublin*, p. 113.

3   *Ibid.*, p. 118.

4   *In Flags or Flitters*, RTÉ television documentary, 1991.

5   www.archiseek.com (accessed 2014).

6   CFP, Paddy Flynn, in an interview with Kathleen O'Connor, 1983, courtesy of George Pujolas.

7   *IT*, 15 June 1963.

8   *Ibid.*, 11 November 2006.

9   RTÉ *Liveline* programme, 22 November 2013.

10   'The Enchanted Palace' by Benedict Kiely was published in *The Bell*, Vol. XVII, No. I, February 1952, pp. 34–43: 'She repelled the suggestion that she frequently attended the cinema as sharply as if he had accused her of drinking herself hoarse and blue in the face every night in Mulligan's pub.'

11   *The Blade*, Toledo, Ohio, 26 November 1967.

12   *II*, 6 March 1968; *IP*, 8 March 1968.

13   *IP*, 28 March 1968.

14   ROD, Mulligan's (Poolbeg Street) 1968–85–162.

15   Byrne earned the nickname having once worked in the Johnston, Mooney and O'Brien bakery, which makes Butterkrust bread.

16   Paddy Madden's article supplied to the author by Peter Roche.

7   Barometer

1   Recollection of William 'Spud' Murphy, in conversation with the author, 2014.

2   Tim Pat Coogan, *A Memoir* (2008), p. 145.

3   Paddy Madden, 'Mulligan's – a pub that sends your soul on

holiday', special souvenir poster, supplied to the author by Peter Roche.

4   Ger Cusack, in an interview with the author, 2014.

5   P. J. (Paddy) Kelly, in an interview with the author, 2014. Paddy Kelly left his native Kilbeggan, County Westmeath, at sixteen years of age, for Dublin and began serving his time as a barman. He fulfilled various roles from apprentice to leaseholder. He was one of the city's best known bartenders, having worked in Taylor's of Swords, O'Donoghue's, Suffolk Street, Mooney's, Abbey Street, the Silver Granite in Palmerstown, and Carthy's, Drumcondra. After his lease was up in Carthy's he met Con Cusack by chance in O'Connell Street and, with a bit of persuasion, he began in Mulligan's while one of the staff went on holiday. The arrangement was meant to be temporary but when a permanent position came up, Con Cusack persuaded Paddy to take it and he remained there for twelve years until he retired.

6   Brigid Cusack, in an interview with the author, 2014. The couple moved out to a house in Clontarf, a suburb on the north side of Dublin, in 1991.

7   Peter Roche, in an interview with the author, 2014.

8   *IP*, 16 April 1970.

9   *Ibid.*, 25 November 1970.

10 Recollection of Patrick O'Brien, in conversation with the author, 2014.

11 *Catholic Herald*, 16 March 1990.

12 O'Toole, *More Kicks Than Pence*, p. 13.

13 Aodhan Madden, *Fear and Loathing in Dublin* (2009), pp. 8–9.

14 Recollection of Tim Pat Coogan. Cregan was an uncle of the celebrated Limerick hurler, Éamonn Cregan.

15 *IT*, 16 December 1971.

8 A Tribute to Con

1 *The Kerryman*, 13 January 1989, in a profile reproduced from *In Dublin*.

2 *Ibid.*

3 *Waiting for Houlihan*, produced and directed by Maurice Healy (Imagine Films, 2012).

4 *Ibid.*

5 *SI*, 5 August 2012.

6 *The Kerryman*, 13 January 1989, in a profile reproduced from *In Dublin*.

7 *Waiting for Houlihan*, produced and directed by Maurice Healy (Imagine Films, 2012).

8 *EP*, 17 September 1978. The final score was: Dublin 0–9, Kerry 5–11.

9 Charles Haughey (1925–2006), as leader of Fianna Fáil, was appointed taoiseach (prime minister) of Ireland three times. He is credited with transforming the Irish economy in the late 1980s, but his career and reputation were damaged by a succession of scandals.

10 *EH*, 15 April 2009.

11 *The Kerryman*, 13 January 1989, in a profile reproduced from *In Dublin*.

12 *Ibid.*

13 *Ibid.*

14 *IE*, 11 August 2012.

15 *IT*, 9 August 2012.

16 *II*, 23 February 2013.

17 *Ibid.*, 16 February 2013.

18 P. J. (Paddy) Kelly, in an interview with the author, 2014.

19 *II*, 23 February 2013.

20 *Ibid.*, 16 March 2013.

21 *Ibid.*, 13 February 2008.

22 *Ibid.*

23 Recollection of Tomás Ó Duinn, in conversation with the author, 1993.

9 Double Century

1   The Troubles is a term used to describe the conflict in Northern Ireland that began in the late 1960s, and is considered by many to have ended with the signing of the Good Friday Agreement (also known as the Belfast Agreement) in 1998.

2   Recollection of former *Irish Press* employees, Cyril Byrne and Fergal Kearns, in conversations with the author, 2014. The *Irish Press* offices continued to be the subject of bomb alerts in the late 1970s and early 1980s.

3   Based on a recollection of Tom Wall, in conversation with the author, 2014.

4   *IT*, 6 March 1975.

5   *IP*, 11 May 1976.

6   *IT*, 24 December 1977.

7   *Magill*, 2 March 1978.

8   Christy Hynes, in an interview with the author, 2014.

9   Noel Hawkins, in an interview with the author, 2014.

10   *Ibid.*

11   *Ibid.*

12   *Ibid.*

13   Dave and Mike Carr, Jon and Siobhan Monroe and Peter Kilbride, in communications to the author, 2014.

14   Noel Hawkins, in an interview with the author, 2014.

15   *In Dublin*, 17 April 1980.

16   *IP*, 16 June 1982.

17   *The New York Times*, 17 June 1982.

18   Galway defeated Mayo 1–13 to 1–10.

19   *II*, 14 January 2003.

20   Gary Cusack, in an interview with the author, 2014.

21   Paul Williams, *Badfellas* (2011), pp. 196–198.

22   *IT*, 17 August 1983.

23   CFP, Paddy Flynn, in an interview with Kathleen O'Connor 1983, courtesy of George Pujolas.

10 Mulligan's in Print

1   *IT*, 7 April 1988.

2   Noel Hawkins, in an interview with the author, 2014.

3   Ger Cusack, in an interview with the author, 2014.

4   Recollection of Ray Cullen, in conversation with the author, 2014.

5   *Barfly* magazine, July 1995.

6   *IT*, 7 April 1988.

7   *Ibid.*, 5 October 1984.

8   Pete St. John, *Jaysus Wept* (1984), p. 5.

9   *Ibid.*, p. 26.

10 *Ibid.*, p. 6.

11 A. P. Kearns, in an interview with the author, 2014.

12 William 'Spud' Murphy, in an interview with the author, 2014. The card game, Don, shortened from Pedro Dom (the name applied to the five of trumps from the game Pedro) involves four players in partnerships who receive nine cards each from a fifty-two-card pack.

13 Joyce, *Ulysses*, p. 83.

14 *IP*, 9 May 1986.

15 P. J. (Paddy) Kelly, in an interview with the author, 2014.

16 Christy Hynes, in an interview with the author, 2014. Christy, who is from Inchicore, had worked in the Rendezvous (now the Beaumont House) in Beaumont, Dublin, and in the Black Sheep in Coolock, Dublin.

17 *Ibid.*

18 *Ibid.*

19 John Horgan, in a foreword to Ray Burke's *Press Delete* (2005), p. 18.

20 Burke, *Press Delete*, pp. 29–30.

21 *II*, 16 April 2008.

22 *Hospitality Ireland*, October/November 2003.

23 *Ibid.*

24 Peter Roche and Billy Phelan, in interviews with the author, 2014.

25 *Hospitality Ireland,* October/November 2003.

26 *Ibid.*

27 P. J. (Paddy) Kelly, in an interview with the author, 2014.

28 *Ulster Herald,* 16 May 1992.

11 Press Closes

1   *IP*, 23 July 1990.

2   *Ibid.*, 28 November 1990.

3   *IT*, 3 December 1990.

4   P. J. (Paddy) Kelly, in an interview with the author, 2014.

5   *IP*, 28 September 1990. *Schindler's Ark* was later turned into a screenplay with the title *Schindler's List.* The book Keneally was writing at the time was *Now and in Time to Be: Ireland and the Irish* (1991).

6   *LMU, The Magazine of the Loyola Marymount University*, 30 August 2013, quoted in an article by its editor, Joseph Wakelee-Lynch.

7   Gary Cusack, in an interview with the author, 2014.

8   Martin Mannion, in a communication to the author, 2014.

9   *II*, 15 June 1991.

10 Christy Hynes, in an interview with the author, 2014.

11 *IP*, 24 July 1991.

12 *Ibid.*, 25 July 1991.

13 Gary Cusack, in an interview with the author, 2014.

14 *Ibid.*, 2014. Gary also recounted another unexplained phenomenon that he experienced in January 2014: 'I was on my own
in the pub and I went downstairs to get a crate of big bottles of
white lemonade. They are at the back. The light wasn't working.
I knew where they were and I could feel something going
right across me. The little light that was there was blocked
momentarily as something brushed past me. It was only for a
split second.'

15 Christy Hynes, in an interview with the author, 2014.

16 *IT*, 4 October 2002.

17 Gary Cusack, in an interview with the author, 2014. O'Hare
was arrested by gardaí in Dundalk in County Louth, on 24
August 1973 and charged before the Special Criminal Court
with membership of the IRA. On 2 October O'Hare was
convicted of the offence and sentenced to twelve months
in prison. Three IRA inmates, Kevin Mallon, J. B. O'Hagan
and Seamus Twomey escaped from the prison by helicopter
twenty-nine days later. O'Hare was one of four defendants
later convicted on 19 June 1974 of aiding and abetting by force
the escape of Twomey. All were sentenced to twelve months in
prison for this offence.

18 *II*, 30 January 1990.

19 *Ibid.*, 5 August 1991.

20 *IP*, 1 May 1992.

21 *Ibid.*, 28 July 1992.

22 *The Boston Globe*, 21 February 1993.

23 *II*, 20 August 1994.

24 *IT*, 3 April 1992.

25 *IP*, 3 March 1993.

26 *Ibid.*, 6 September 1993. All three were accomplished hurlers. Irwin had lined out for St Finbarr's Club in Cork. Quinn is a former Dublin minor player. While Moran is best remembered for his prowess as a Gaelic footballer, he also played hurling.

27 Billy Phelan, quoted in *Hospitality Ireland*, October/November 2003.

28 *SI*, 16 April 2006.

29 *II*, 2 March 2013.

30 *SP*, 19 June 1994.

31 *IT*, 22 June 1994. Christy Hynes described the split shift that had operated before the settlement was agreed: 'You started at 10.30 in the morning and then you went home at 12.30 and you came back at 2 p.m. You went off again at 5.30 and you came back at 7 p.m. and you were there for the night. That was one of the shifts. You would do that every day except your two days off. You had one long day, you went at 1.30 p.m. and came back at 7 p.m. I think that was every fortnight. We put in long hours. That changed around 1994 during the barmen's strike. That was a huge victory, better than money.'

32 Recollection of Billy 'Swiss' Phelan, in an interview with the author, 2014.

33 *IP*, 2 September 1994.

34 The 'Night Town' reporter was the overnight reporter. James Joyce took the word from the Dublin newspapers and used it as 'Nighttown' in *Ulysses*. The word is still used on Dublin newspapers.

35 Myles McEntee, in conversation with the author, 2014.

36 Frank Kilfeather, *Changing Times – A Life in Journalism* (1997).

37 Recollection of Vincent Reddin, in conversation with the author, 2014.

12 A New Century

1 *IT*, 25 July 1995.

2 Peter Roche, in an interview with the author, 2014.

3 *The Irish Echo*, 2 August 1995.

4 Peter Roche, in an interview with the author, 2014.

5 P. J. (Paddy) Kelly interview with the author, 2014.

6 Christy Hynes, in an interview with the author, 2014.

7 *Sunday World*, 11 October 1998. McGovern died on 21 June 1998.

8 *SI*, 16 April 2006.

9 Ger Cusack, in an interview with the author, 2014.

10 Christy Hynes, in an interview with the author, 2014.

11 *II*, 29 June 1999.

12 The new law came into effect on 6 July 2000.

13 Danny Tracey, in an interview with the author, 2014.

14 Talbot Fyan had brought his children in to help out with his spirit grocery in the late 1790s, and John Mulligan, in turn, set his son James to assist him in the 1860s. James's daughter, Mary, followed suit in the late 1890s. Michael Smith hired his nephews Con and Tommie Cusack in the mid-twentieth century, and Tommie's sons, Gary and Ger, were also brought in to learn the bar business at an early age.

15 *II*, 24 November 2001.

16 Danny Tracey, in an interview with the author, 2014.

17 Billy Phelan, in an interview with the author, 2014. Bennett was introduced to the theatre by the *Irish Press* theatre critic, Michael Sheridan, in Mulligan's in 1972. In an interview with the *Leitrim Observer*, 28 December 1994, Bennett said that Sheridan cast him in a play he was directing after he had heard him telling yarns in the pub.

18 Danny Tracey, in an interview with the author, 2014.

19 *SI*, 16 April 2006.

20 *IT*, 25 March 2006.

21 Billy Phelan, in an interview with the author, 2014. *The Exonerated*, by Jessica Blank and Erik Jensen, ran at the Liberty Hall Theatre 10–14 October 2006.

22 www.dit.ie, accessed 2014.

23 Darran Cusack, in an interview with the author, 2014. Darran attended the Dublin Institute of Technology, where he completed a two-year course in Bar Management and Entrepreneurship.

24 Public Broadcasting Service (United States), *Historic Pubs of Dublin* (2008).

25 Thomas Kennedy, *Dark Drink and Conversations* (2008); and *More Dark Drink and Conversations* (2009).

26 Bill Barich, *A Pint of Plain: Tradition, Change and the Fate of the Irish Pub* (2009).

27 *Ibid.*, pp. 128–134.

28 Mike Carr, in a communication to the author, 2014.

29 *Ibid.*

30 Peter Roche, in conversation with the author, 2014. Houlihan died on 4 August 2012.

31 *II*, 20 April 2013.

32 *Quirke* is a British–Irish crime drama television series that was first broadcast on BBC One and RTÉ One in 2014. The three-part series is based on the books by John Banville, writing under the pseudonym Benjamin Black, and was adapted by Andrew Davies and Conor McPherson. It stars Gabriel Byrne and Michael Gambon.

33 *Ripper Street* stars Matthew Macfadyen, Jerome Flynn and Adam Rothenberg. The first episode was broadcast on 30 December 2012. It began to air in the USA on BBC America on 19 January 2013. Its production designer, Mark Geraghty, works in Ireland and internationally for acclaimed directors such as Kevin Reynolds, Mike Newell, Jim Sheridan and Stephen Frears. He trained in Ireland, working on *The Commitments*, *My Left Foot* and *Into the West*, among others.

34 *SI*, 16 April 2006.

BIBLIOGRAPHY

Archives

Dublin City Library and Archive

Dublin Diocesan Archives

General Register Office, Dublin

Glasnevin Trust

Irish Architectural Archive

Irish Film Archive

Irish Times Digital Archive

Licensed Vintners Association Archive

National Library of Ireland

RTÉ Archives

Registry of Deeds, Dublin

Newspapers and magazines

The Barfly, The Blade (Ohio), The Boston Globe, Catholic Herald, Connacht Tribune, Connaught Telegraph, Evening Herald, Evening Press, The Freeman's Journal, Hospitality Ireland, In Dublin, The Irish Echo, The Irish Examiner, Irish Independent, The Irish Press, The Irish Times, The Kerryman, Leitrim Observer, Limerick Leader, Limerick Observer, Look, Loyola Marymount University magazine, Magill, Meath Chronicle, The New York Times, Sunday Independent, The Sunday Press, Sunday Review, Sunday World, Ulster Herald, Xpress

Directories

*Thom's Irish Almanac and Official Directory (*Alexander Thom & Co.)

Dublin Almanac (Pettigrew and Oulton)

Pigot's Commercial Directory of Ireland

The Treble Almanac: Wilson's Dublin Directory

Websites

www.mulligansbook.com

www.archiseek.com

www.iarc.ie

www.irishnewsarchive.com

www.irishtimes.com

www.johnboland.ie

www.mulligans.ie

www.rootsireland.ie

Articles, collections, reports etc.

Buckley, Laureen, 'Tara Street/Poolbeg Street Skeletal Report' (1992) (NMSA)

Channing, John, 'Report on Archaeological Monitoring and Excavations at Poolbeg, Dublin 2' (1992) (NMSA)

Journals of the House of Lords, Vol. CIV (London, 1872), p. 737

Kiely, Benedict, 'The Enchanted Palace', *The Bell*, Vol. XVII, No. I, February 1952, pp. 34–43

O'Brien, Flann, 'The trade in Dublin', *The Bell*, Vol. I, No. 2, November 1940, pp. 6–15

Reynolds, Mairéad, 'James Donovan, Dublin china merchants', *Irish Arts Review*, Vol. 2, No. 3 (1985), pp. 28–36

Roddy, Joseph, 'They cried the rain down that night', *Look*, Vol. 28, No. 23, 17 November 1964, pp. 75–83

Books

Barich, Bill, *A Pint of Plain: Tradition, Change and the Fate of the Irish Pub* (London, 2009)

Berry, Henry F., *A History of the Royal Dublin Society* (London, 1915)

Burke, Ray, *Press Delete* (Dublin, 2005)

Cobbett, William, *Cobbett's Annual Register*, July to September 1802, Vol. II (London, 1803)

Coogan, Tim Pat, *A Memoir* (London, 2008)

Craig, Maurice, *Dublin 1660–1860: The Shaping of the City* (Dublin, 1980)

Davis, Thomas, *The Speeches of the Rt. Hon. John Philpot Curran* (Dublin, 1868)

Donnelly, Nicholas N., *History of Dublin Parishes*, Vol. II (Dublin, 1910)

Ellmann, Richard (ed.), *Letters of James Joyce*, Vol. II (New York, 1966)

Ellmann, Richard, *James Joyce* (London, 1982)

Gerold, Frank, *Judy* (Cambridge, Mass., USA, 1999)

Hopkins, Frank, *Hidden Dublin: Deadbeats, Dossers and Decent Skins* (Cork, 2007)

Jones Howell, Thomas, *A Complete Collection of State Trials and Proceedings for High Treason*, Vol. XXVII (London, 1820)

Joyce, James, *Ulysses* (Penguin edn, London 1992)

Joyce, James, *Dubliners* (London, 2013)

Kearns, Kevin C., *Dublin Pub Life and Lore – An Oral History* (Niwot, Col., USA, 1997)

Kelly, Bill, *Me Darlin' Dublin's Dead and Gone* (Dublin, 1983)

Kennedy, Thomas, *Dark Drink and Conversations* (Dublin, 2008)

Kennedy, Thomas, *More Dark Drink and Conversations* (Dublin, 2009)

Kilfeather, Frank, *Changing Times – A Life in Journalism* (Dublin, 1997)

Lennon, Colm, *Irish Historic Towns Atlas, No. 19: Dublin, Part II, 1610 to 1756* (Dublin, 2008)

MacThomáis, Éamonn, *The Labour and the Royal* (Dublin, 1979)

Madden, Aodhan, *Fear and Loathing in Dublin* (Dublin, 2009)

O'Donovan, John (ed.), *Annals of the Kingdoms of Ireland by the Four Masters* (Dublin, 1854)

Ó Laoi, Pádraic, *Nora Barnacle Joyce: A Portrait* (Galway, 1982)

O'Toole, Michael, *More Kicks Than Pence* (Dublin, 1992)

Ryan, Philip B., *The Lost Theatres of Dublin* (Westbury, 1998)

Smyrl, Steven C., *Dictionary of Dublin Dissent – Dublin's Protestant Dissenting Meeting Houses, 1660–1920* (Dublin, 2009)

St. John, Pete, *Jaysus Wept* (Birr, 1984)

Strickland, Walter G., *A Dictionary of Irish Artists*, Vol. II (Dublin and London, 1913)

Usher, Dr Robin, *Protestant Dublin, 1660–1760: Architecture and Iconography* (Basingstoke, UK and New York, 2012)

Whitelaw, Rev. James, *An Essay on the Population of Dublin* (Dublin, 1805)

Williams, Paul, *Badfellas* (Dublin, 2011)

Wright, Rev. G. N., *An Historical Guide to Ancient and Modern Dublin* (London, 1821)

INDEX

BY THE SAME AUTHOR

PETER'S KEY

Peter DeLoughry and the
Fight for Irish Independence

ISBN: 978 1 78117 059 5

€19.99

In February 1919 three Irish prisoners, most notably Éamon de Valera, broke out of Lincoln jail without having to dig a tunnel or fire a shot. The escape was the culmination of months of planning, but it would have been impossible without one man – Peter DeLoughry. In *Peter's Key* DeLoughry emerges from the shadow of his more famous fellow inmate. The book also sheds new light on the bitter disagreements involving members of the Kilkenny Brigade and Ernie O'Malley, as well as revealing the fractious relationship that developed between DeLoughry on one side and de Valera and Harry Boland on the other. DeLoughry was also mayor of Kilkenny for six consecutive years, served in the first Seanad, and was a Cumann na nGaedheal TD. Relying on previously unpublished material, Declan Dunne, DeLoughry's grandson, tells the story of a man who played a critical role in the story of Ireland's independence.

www.mercierpress.ie

MERCIER PRESS

IRISH PUBLISHER - IRISH STORY

We hope you enjoyed this book.

Since 1944, Mercier Press has published books that have been critically important to Irish life and culture.

Our website is the best place to find out more information about Mercier, our books, authors, news and the best deals on a wide variety of books. Mercier tracks the best prices for our books online and we seek to offer the best value to our customers, offering free delivery within Ireland.

A large selection of Mercier's new releases and backlist are also available as ebooks. We have an ebook for everyone, with titles available for the Amazon Kindle, Sony Reader, Kobo Reader, Apple products and many more. Visit our website to find and buy our ebooks.

Sign up on our website or complete and return the form below to receive updates and special offers.

www.mercierpress.ie
www.facebook.com/mercier.press
www.twitter.com/irishpublisher

Name: _____

Email: _____

Address: _____

Mobile No.: _____

Mercier Press, Unit 3b, Oak House, Bessboro Rd, Blackrock, Cork, Ireland